SUBSTANCE ABUSE ASSESSMENT, INTERVENTIONS AND TREATMENT

PRESCRIPTION DRUGS

ABUSE EDUCATION AND DIVERSION CONTROL EFFORTS

SUBSTANCE ABUSE ASSESSMENT, INTERVENTIONS AND TREATMENT

Additional books in this series can be found on Nova's website under the Series tab.

Additional E-books in this series can be found on Nova's website under the E-books tab.

SUBSTANCE ABUSE ASSESSMENT, INTERVENTIONS AND TREATMENT

PRESCRIPTION DRUGS

ABUSE EDUCATION AND DIVERSION CONTROL EFFORTS

JOHN J. PHILLIPS
AND
WALLACE O. PENNY
EDITORS

Nova Science Publishers, Inc.
New York

For permission to use material from this book please contact us:
Telephone 631-231-7269; Fax 631-231-8175
Web Site: http://www.novapublishers.com

Library of Congress Cataloging-in-Publication Data

ISBN 978-1-62081-211-2

Published by Nova Science Publishers, Inc. † New York

Contents

PREFACE

The Center for Disease Control and Prevention has declared that the United States is in the midst of an epidemic of prescription drug overdose deaths, with deaths associated to prescription pain relievers of particular concern. To address this issue, federal agencies are raising awareness by educating prescribers and the general public. This book examines the recent national trends in prescription pain reliever abuse and misuse; describes how the federal agencies are educating prescribers; assesses the extent to which federal agencies follow key practices for developing public education efforts; and identifies educational efforts that use similar strategies and assesses how agencies coordinate those efforts.

Chapter 1 – The Centers for Disease Control and Prevention has declared that the United States is in the midst of an epidemic of prescription drug overdose deaths, with deaths associated with prescription pain relievers of particular concern. To address this issue, federal agencies are raising awareness by educating prescribers and the general public. In response to your request, GAO (1) described recent national trends in prescription pain reliever abuse and misuse, (2) described how federal agencies are educating prescribers, (3) assessed the extent to which federal agencies follow key practices for developing public education efforts, and (4) identified educational efforts that use similar strategies and assessed how agencies coordinate those efforts.

GAO interviewed officials and reviewed documents and websites from seven agencies involved in federal drug control efforts and analyzed the most recent data from several data sources related to prescription pain reliever abuse and misuse. GAO also assessed the development of public education efforts and federal coordination efforts against key practices from prior GAO work.

Chapter 2 – The Drug Enforcement Administration's (DEA) Diversion Control Program is responsible for enforcing the Controlled Substances Act (CSA) and ensuring the availability of prescription drugs such as pain relievers and stimulants while preventing their diversion for abuse. The CSA requires entities handling controlled substances—such as manufacturers, pharmacies, and physicians, among others-- to register with DEA, which conducts regulatory investigations of registrants, as well as criminal investigations. GAO was asked (1) how DEA manages diversion investigation efforts, and (2) how DEA ensures policies and procedures are followed for investigations and the extent to which it determines the results of its efforts. GAO reviewed DEA policies and procedures, and interviewed DEA, state, and local officials at eleven locations which were selected on the basis of volume of cases handled, geographic diversity, and other considerations. These observations are not generalizable, but provided insights on DEA operations.

Chapter 3 - The diversion and abuse of pharmaceutical controlled substances is a significant and growing problem in the United States. Leading indicators show substantially high levels in the abuse and misuse (non-medical use) of these drugs and the consequences associated with such actions. These indicators include, but are not limited to: the National Survey on Drug Use and Health, Monitoring the Future Study, Partnership Attitude Tracking Study (PATS), Drug Abuse Warning Network (DAWN) data, Treatment Episode Data Set, American Poison Control Centers data, and the National Forensic Laboratory Information System (NFLIS).

Chapter 4 - The PMP Center of Excellence seeks to help end the prescription drug abuse epidemic in the United States without compromising accepted standards of pain management or the legitimate prescribing of controlled substances. In collaboration with the Alliance of States with Prescription Monitoring Programs, the Center provides academically sound and practice-relevant information, evaluation, and expertise to PMPs and their stakeholders. The Center is funded by a grant from the Department of Justice Bureau of Justice Assistance.

Their work is focused on helping PMPs identify and implement the most effective means possible for them to intervene in the prescription drug abuse epidemic.

In: Prescription Drugs
Editors: J. J. Phillips and W. O. Penny
ISBN 978-1-62081-211-2

Chapter 1

PRESCRIPTION PAIN RELIEVER ABUSE: AGENCIES HAVE BEGUN COORDINATING EDUCATION EFFORTS, BUT NEED TO ASSESS EFFECTIVENESS*

United States Government Accountability Office

WHY GAO DID THIS STUDY

The Centers for Disease Control and Prevention has declared that the United States is in the midst of an epidemic of prescription drug overdose deaths, with deaths associated with prescription pain relievers of particular concern. To address this issue, federal agencies are raising awareness by educating prescribers and the general public. In response to your request, GAO (1) described recent national trends in prescription pain reliever abuse and misuse, (2) described how federal agencies are educating prescribers, (3) assessed the extent to which federal agencies follow key practices for developing public education efforts, and (4) identified educational efforts that use similar strategies and assessed how agencies coordinate those efforts.

GAO interviewed officials and reviewed documents and websites from seven agencies involved in federal drug control efforts and analyzed the most

* This is an edited, reformatted and augmented version of a United States Government Accountability Office Publication No. GAO-12-115, dated December 2011.

recent data from several data sources related to prescription pain reliever abuse and misuse. GAO also assessed the development of public education efforts and federal coordination efforts against key practices from prior GAO work.

What GAO Recommends

GAO recommends that the Director of ONDCP establish outcome metrics and implement a plan to evaluate proposed educational efforts, and ensure that agencies share lessons learned among similar efforts. ONDCP did not explicitly agree or disagree with GAO's recommendations, but noted that it will continue to work for improved coordination of educational efforts and evaluation of outcomes.

What GAO Found

Key measures of prescription pain reliever abuse and misuse increased from 2003 to 2009. The largest increases were in measures of adverse health consequences such as emergency department visits, substance abuse treatment admissions, and unintentional overdose deaths, though increases were not consistent across all measures. Federal officials suggested that increasing availability of prescription pain relievers and high-risk behaviors by those who abuse or misuse the drugs, such as combining prescription pain relievers with other drugs or alcohol, likely contributed to the rise in adverse health consequences, though data about the reasons for the increases are limited.

The Food and Drug Administration (FDA), the National Institutes of Health (NIH), and the Substance Abuse and Mental Health Services Administration (SAMHSA) use a variety of strategies to educate prescribers about issues related to prescription pain reliever abuse and misuse, but officials told us that more education is needed. The strategies used include developing continuing medical education programs, requiring training and certification in order to prescribe certain drugs, and developing curriculum resources for future prescribers. The Office of National Drug Control Policy (ONDCP) is working to develop a legislative proposal to require education for prescribers registering with the Drug Enforcement Administration (DEA) to prescribe controlled substances. Officials from some agencies said such a requirement would ensure all prescribers were starting from the same baseline of knowledge.

In their efforts to educate the public about prescription pain reliever abuse and misuse, DEA, FDA, NIH, ONDCP, and SAMHSA used almost all of the key practices for developing their consumer education efforts. Agencies varied in how they used the key practices when developing these efforts, which varied in size, scope, and duration. All agencies established metrics to monitor the implementation and functional elements of their educational efforts, but only two agencies have established or are planning to establish metrics to assess the impact of their efforts on audiences' knowledge, attitudes, and behavior. Without outcome evaluations, federal agencies have limited knowledge of how effective their efforts are in achieving their goals—in this case, reducing prescription pain reliever abuse and misuse.

Among federal initiatives to educate prescribers and the public about prescription pain reliever abuse and misuse, GAO found several instances of agencies engaging in similar efforts, directed at similar target audiences and using similar mediums. Officials said that these similarities in public education efforts are beneficial in addressing prescription drug abuse and misuse because having multiple, reinforcing messages about the same subject is valuable in public health communications and because federal agencies provide slightly different perspectives on the issues surrounding prescription drug abuse and misuse. Likewise, the prescriber education programs GAO identified, though similar, are different in content and focus. Though these similar programs have the potential to be duplicative if not effectively coordinated, federal agencies have recently begun to coordinate their educational efforts. Nevertheless, federal agencies have missed opportunities to share lessons learned and pool resources among similar education efforts.

ABBREVIATIONS

APQ	aggregate production quota
CDC	Centers for Disease Control and Prevention
CE	continuing education
CME	continuing medical education
DAWN	Drug Abuse Warning Network
DEA	Drug Enforcement Administration
FDA	Food and Drug Administration
HHS	Department of Health and Human Services

HRSA	Health Resources and Services Administration
NIDA	National Institute on Drug Abuse
NIH	National Institutes of Health
NSDUH	National Survey on Drug Use and Health
NVSS	National Vital Statistics System
ONDCP	Office of National Drug Control Policy
REMS	Risk Evaluation and Mitigation Strategy
SAMHSA	Substance Abuse and Mental Health Services Administration
TEDS	Treatment Episode Data Set

December 22, 2011
The Honorable Darrell Issa Chairman
Committee on Oversight and Government Reform
House of Representatives
The Honorable Mary Bono Mack
House of Representatives
The Honorable Edolphus Towns
House of Representatives

The Centers for Disease Control and Prevention (CDC) has declared that the United States is in the midst of an epidemic of prescription drug overdose deaths, with such drugs involved in more overdose deaths than those involving heroin and cocaine combined. Further, according to CDC, recent increases in prescription drug overdose deaths overall are largely driven by deaths associated with prescription pain relievers, which include such drugs as OxyContin or Vicodin, among others.

In 2009, an estimated 12.4 million Americans reported using a prescription pain reliever in the past year without a prescription of their own or simply for the experience or feeling the drug caused, according to the National Survey on Drug Use and Health (NSDUH). Seventy percent of these people reported that they got the drug from a friend or family member, while another 19 percent got the drug from a doctor.[1]

Although specific regions of the country have been severely affected by this problem, recent media reports from across the United States suggest it is now a national issue.

Multiple federal agencies have responsibility for addressing the abuse and misuse of prescription pain relievers through prevention, treatment, and enforcement activities.[2,3] The Office of National Drug Control Policy

(ONDCP) assists in setting national drug control priorities and helps to coordinate federal drug control efforts. One prevention activity ONDCP has identified as a focus area is raising awareness of the problem of prescription drug abuse and misuse through the education of parents, youth, patients, and health care providers.

Accordingly, the Drug Enforcement Administration (DEA), the Food and Drug Administration (FDA), the Health Resources and Services Administration (HRSA), the National Institutes of Health's (NIH) National Institute on Drug Abuse (NIDA), the Substance Abuse and Mental Health Services Administration (SAMHSA), and ONDCP are engaged in various activities for educating the public and health care providers who prescribe pain relievers about issues related to abuse and misuse of these drugs.

These federal agencies and ONDCP (hereinafter collectively referred to as "federal agencies") have assisted in developing and implementing strategies specifically focused on preventing the inappropriate use of prescription pain relievers since the early 2000s, and our prior reports have documented some of their efforts.[4]

You asked us to update our prior work on OxyContin to reflect changes in oxycodone abuse trends and efforts aimed at stemming prescription drug abuse since our 2003 report. In response to that request, we (1) describe recent national trends in prescription pain reliever abuse and misuse, (2) describe how federal agencies are educating prescribers about prescription pain reliever abuse and misuse, (3) assess the extent to which federal agencies follow key practices for developing public education efforts about prescription pain reliever abuse and misuse, and (4) identify educational efforts that use similar strategies and assess how agencies coordinate those efforts.

At your request, we also provide information on manufacturer-initiated efforts to develop abuse-deterrent formulations of prescription pain relievers (see app. I) and DEA's process for setting quotas for certain substances used in the manufacture of prescription pain relievers (see app. II).

To describe recent national trends in prescription pain reliever abuse and misuse, we interviewed officials from CDC, DEA, FDA, NIH, ONDCP, and SAMHSA; conducted a literature review to identify relevant data sources and explanations for trends in prescription pain reliever abuse and misuse; and analyzed data related to prescription pain reliever abuse and misuse from several data sources representative of the U.S. population aged 12 years and older.

We included data in our review from the Drug Abuse Warning Network (DAWN), NSDUH, the National Vital Statistics System (NVSS), and the

Treatment Episode Data Set (TEDS). We selected these four data sources because they are the data sources that the responsible agencies use for monitoring trends in prescription pain reliever abuse and misuse, and because they are nationally representative.

We analyzed data for calendar years 2003 to 2009, the most recent years for which data from at least three data sources were available. (See app. III for more information about these data sources.) To assess the reliability of these data for our purposes, we reviewed related documentation and conducted interviews with knowledgeable agency officials from CDC and SAMHSA to learn about data collection, quality control, and any limitations of these data sources. We also conducted electronic and manual data testing to ensure the quality of the data. We determined that all data we assessed were sufficiently reliable to provide overall trends for the purposes of our review.

To describe how federal agencies are educating prescribers about prescription pain reliever abuse and misuse, we reviewed documents and interviewed officials from FDA, NIH, and SAMHSA to identify and describe educational strategies used during fiscal year 2011. Because they are involved in federal prevention efforts, we also interviewed officials from DEA, HRSA, ONDCP, and the American Medical Association to gain their perspective on gaps in current prescriber education and efforts to fill these gaps.

We excluded agencies that support their own health care systems, such as the Bureau of Prisons, Department of Defense, Indian Health Service, and Department of Veterans Affairs, from the scope of our review as they serve special populations, rather than the general public. We also excluded educational efforts related to drug abuse treatment, including education about the use of the prescription pain relievers methadone or buprenorphine for the treatment of opioid addiction.

To assess the extent to which federal agencies follow key practices for developing public education efforts about prescription pain reliever abuse and misuse, we reviewed agency websites and interviewed officials from DEA, FDA, NIH, SAMHSA, and ONDCP to identify educational efforts. We then assessed the development of those educational efforts against key practices for developing consumer education efforts identified in our prior work.[5]

We limited our scope to efforts that target the general public, rather than special populations, such as educational efforts pursued by the Department of Veterans Affairs, Department of Defense, or Indian Health Service. We also focused on efforts that were being actively revised or disseminated in fiscal year 2011. Finally, we focused on efforts that craft targeted messages about abuse and misuse, rather than efforts that strictly provide factual information, such as a limited number of drug fact websites, since our criteria for developing consumer education efforts are only appropriate for efforts that seek to convey a particular message.

To identify educational efforts that use similar strategies and assess how agencies coordinate those efforts, we first assessed the extent to which agencies targeted similar populations, provided similar information, and used similar educational strategies. We then interviewed officials from DEA, FDA, HRSA, NIH, SAMHSA, and ONDCP and reviewed agency documents in order to assess federal agencies' coordination efforts against key practices for collaboration identified in our prior work.[6] (See app. III for a detailed discussion of our methodology.)[7]

We conducted this performance audit from December 2010 through December 2011 in accordance with generally accepted government auditing standards. Those standards require that we plan and perform the audit to obtain sufficient, appropriate evidence to provide a reasonable basis for our findings and conclusions based on our audit objectives. We believe that the evidence obtained provides a reasonable basis for our findings and conclusions based on our audit objectives.

BACKGROUND

Prescription Pain Relievers

Pain, which affects millions of Americans, can be characterized in terms of intensity—mild to severe—and duration—acute or chronic.[8] While the appropriate medical treatment of pain varies according to these two dimensions, opioid analgesics can provide pain relief for some patients. These prescription pain relievers can be made in either immediate-release or extended-release formulations. Immediate-release pain relievers work for shorter periods of time, while extended-release pain relievers are designed to provide a longer period of drug release so that they can be taken less frequently.[9]

Prescription pain relievers are sometimes used in a manner other than as prescribed—that is, they are abused and misused. While federal agencies' definitions of abuse and misuse vary, they generally incorporate three types of inappropriate use. First, some individuals use prescription pain relievers with the intent to get high, whether or not they were prescribed the drugs. Second, some individuals use prescription pain relievers that they were not prescribed to relieve pain; for example, by borrowing a pill from a friend in order to treat a headache.[10] Third, some individuals, while seeking pain relief, incorrectly use prescription pain relievers that were prescribed to them, such as by taking more than prescribed.

Prescription pain relievers have serious risks when they are abused and misused. Abuse and misuse of prescription pain relievers can lead to addiction and severe respiratory depression, which can cause death. Depending on the amount taken, even a single dose could cause death if taken by an individual who does not regularly use such pain relievers and whose body is not accustomed to their effects. Also, using alcohol or other drugs with prescription pain relievers can increase the risk of dangerous side effects, including death.

Preventing Prescription Pain Reliever Abuse and Misuse

Federal agencies use both regulatory and programmatic approaches in their efforts to prevent prescription pain reliever abuse and misuse.[11]

Because of their potential for abuse, prescription pain relievers are regulated under the Controlled Substances Act.[12] Prescribers, such as physicians, physician assistants, nurse practitioners, and dentists, must register with DEA to prescribe drugs regulated under the act, and prescribers serve a key role in reducing prescription drug abuse and misuse.

However, federal agencies have noted gaps in prescriber education about issues related to prescription pain reliever abuse and misuse, including that most prescribers receive little training on the importance of appropriate prescribing and dispensing of prescription pain relievers, on how to recognize substance abuse in their patients, or on treating pain. A recent study on pain education in medical schools found that such education is limited, variable, and often fragmentary.[13]

Further, given the recent introduction of new pain relievers to the U.S. market and advances in pain management, prescribers who completed their medical training in prior years may not have received training in prescribing certain types of pain relievers, such as extended-release or long-acting formulations.

While continuing education of current prescribers could help address this issue, according to an American Medical Association publication, as of September 2011 medical boards in only nine states had a continuing medical education (CME) requirement related to education on controlled substance prescribing or pain management for certain prescribers.[14] A representative of the American Pain Foundation told us that the organization frequently receives reports from patients that, in some communities, prescribers have stopped prescribing prescription pain relievers because of a lack of knowledge about how to safely prescribe them.

Federal public education efforts seek to educate patients and the general public of all ages about the appropriate use, secure storage, and disposal of prescription drugs, as well as the risks associated with prescription drug abuse and misuse (see app. IV for descriptions of federal efforts to educate the general public about prescription pain reliever abuse and misuse).

We have previously identified certain key practices that are important for the development of educational outreach efforts, motivating a target audience, and alleviating challenges, such as prioritizing limited resources.[15]

Federal Agencies Involved in Preventing Prescription Pain Reliever Abuse and Misuse

Multiple federal agencies play a role in preventing the abuse and misuse of prescription pain relievers. Within the Executive Office of the President, ONDCP establishes policies, priorities, and objectives for a national drug control program. ONDCP also oversees several programs related to curbing drug abuse and misuse, including an educational media campaign.

In addition, Department of Health and Human Services (HHS) agencies, including FDA, HRSA, NIH, and SAMHSA, have various responsibilities and engage in activities related to preventing the abuse and misuse of prescription pain relievers.

- FDA is responsible for ensuring the safety and effectiveness of drugs. FDA can require drug manufacturers to take measures to ensure the safety of their products, such as by providing patient and prescriber education materials. FDA also educates patients and providers about appropriate use and potential risks of drugs, including prescription pain relievers, in order to reduce preventable harm from these drugs.
- HRSA operates the federal Poison Control Program, which provides funds for poison control centers that provide treatment recommendations for poisonings involving prescription drug abuse and misuse. This program also has a campaign that includes public education about the risks of poisoning from prescription pain relievers.

- NIH, primarily through its component NIDA, provides strategic support for and conducts research on drug abuse and addiction. NIH's role also includes translating and disseminating this research into materials for public consumption.
- SAMHSA seeks to direct substance abuse and mental health services to the people most in need and promote use of evidence-based practices in these areas in the general health care system. In particular, the agency seeks to educate the public and prescribers about issues related to substance abuse in an effort to prevent such abuse and reduce its prevalence.

Finally, within the Department of Justice, DEA is responsible for enforcing the Controlled Substances Act and related regulations. One of DEA's roles is to control the quantity of schedule I and II controlled substances produced or procured each year in the United States, which it does by establishing annual quotas for U.S. manufacturers. (See app. II for a description of DEA's process for setting quotas for controlled substances.) The agency also supports nonenforcement programs aimed at reducing the illicit use of controlled substances, including education about prescription drug abuse and misuse and diversion.[16]

Federal Data Sources Used to Monitor Prescription Pain Reliever Abuse and Misuse

To monitor trends in the extent of prescription pain reliever abuse and misuse, federal agencies rely on data obtained from four nationally representative data sources. Three of these data sources measure adverse health consequences related to abuse and misuse, and the fourth is a national household survey of drug use.[17]

Although these data sources do not directly measure abuse and misuse, when used together, they provide a more complete view of the problem of prescription pain reliever abuse and misuse than any of the data sources individually.

Therefore, we refer to national data from these four data sources as key measures of prescription pain reliever abuse and misuse. The data sources used by federal agencies are:

- DAWN, a public health surveillance system operated by SAMHSA, collects information on emergency department visits in the United States.
  DAWN staff review emergency department medical records from a nationally representative sample of hospitals to identify and gather information on visits in which drugs were involved, including visits where drugs were a direct cause and visits where drugs were a contributing factor.
- TEDS, compiled by SAMHSA, gathers data from substance abuse treatment facilities in the United States on the demographic characteristics and substance abuse problems of those aged 12 or older admitted for treatment.
- NVSS, operated by CDC, contains vital statistics data, including mortality data, such as causes of death, obtained from death certificates filed for every death from every jurisdiction in the United States.
- NSDUH, an annual household survey sponsored by SAMHSA, gathers self-reported information on the use of illicit drugs (including the "nonmedical use" of prescription drugs), alcohol, and tobacco in the civilian, noninstitutionalized population of the United States aged 12 years old or older.[18]

See appendix III for more information about the data collection methodologies and limitations of these data sources.

KEY MEASURES OF PRESCRIPTION PAIN RELIEVER ABUSE AND MISUSE HAVE INCREASED NATIONWIDE

Key measures of prescription pain reliever abuse and misuse increased from 2003 to 2009.

The largest increases were in measures of adverse health consequences, though increases were not consistent across all measures.

Federal officials suggested that increasing availability of prescription pain relievers and increasing high-risk behaviors by those who abuse or misuse the drugs, such as combining prescription pain relievers with other drugs or alcohol, likely contributed to the rise in adverse health consequences, though data about the reasons for the increases are limited.

Key Measures of Prescription Pain Reliever Abuse and Misuse Increased from 2003 to 2009

Key measures of prescription pain reliever abuse and misuse increased from 2003 to 2009, though increases were not consistent across all measures. All three measures of adverse health consequences that we examined increased substantially in the U.S. population during the period we reviewed (see fig. 1).[19] The estimated number of emergency department visits annually related to prescription pain reliever abuse and misuse increased by 142 percent from 2004 to 2009, an estimated increase of 288,000 visits.[20] Admissions to substance abuse treatment facilities annually for prescription pain reliever abuse and misuse increased by 131 percent, or 133,000 admissions, from 2003 to 2009.[21] The annual number of deaths resulting from unintentional overdoses of prescription pain relievers increased by 83 percent, equivalent to more than 5,000 deaths, from 2003 to 2008.[22]

While these measures of adverse health consequences increased substantially, according to NSDUH survey data, the percent increase in the estimated number of people nationwide who abused and misused prescription pain relievers—another key measure of prescription pain reliever abuse and misuse—was relatively slight during the period we reviewed.[23] In 2003, an estimated 11.7 million people reported abusing or misusing prescription pain relievers at some point over the past year, and this number increased by 6 percent to 12.4 million people in 2009.[24] Appendix V shows data from the key measures by age group for each year that we reviewed.

Increasing Availability and High-Risk Behaviors Likely Contributed to the Increases in Adverse Health Consequences

Although information about the reasons for the substantial increases in adverse health consequences is limited, agency officials suggested that increasing availability of prescription pain relievers, especially extended-release and long-acting pain relievers, and increasing high-risk behaviors by those who abuse or misuse the drugs were likely contributors to the increased adverse health consequences related to prescription pain reliever abuse and misuse from 2003-2009. Over this time period, the number of prescriptions dispensed from U.S. pharmacies for prescription pain relievers increased by 32 percent—from 195 million prescriptions in 2003 to 257 million prescriptions in 2009—which CDC, FDA, and NIH officials attributed to factors such as an

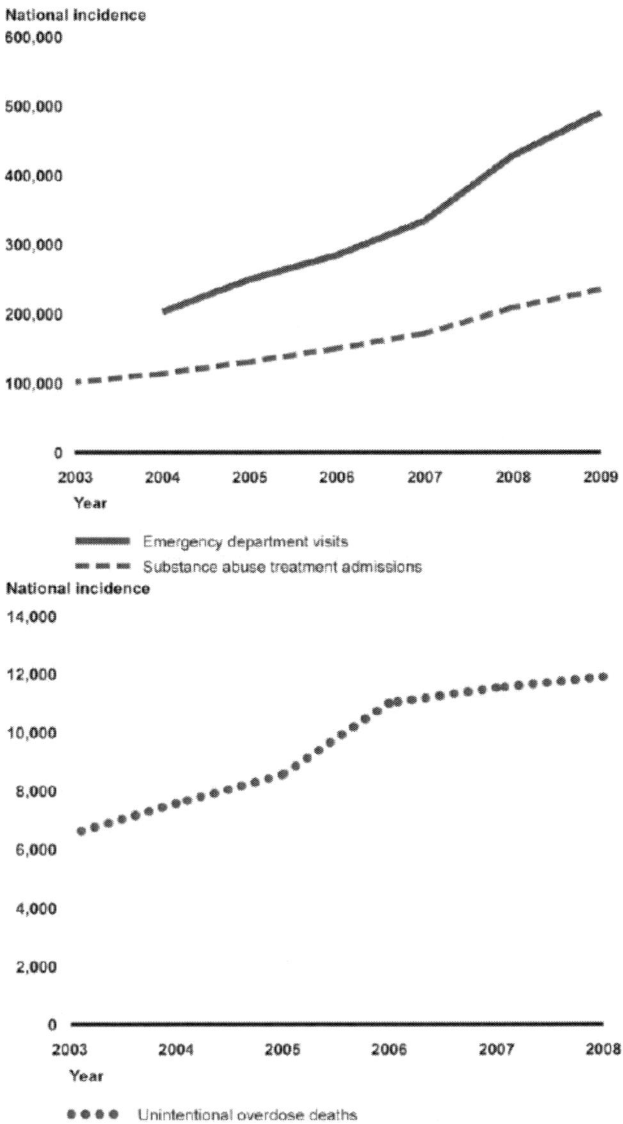

Notes: Comparable emergency department visit estimates are not available for 2003 because changes were made that year to the data collection methodology. Unintentional overdose deaths data from 2009 were not published in time for this report. See app. V for the estimated number of emergency department visits, admissions to substance abuse treatment facilities, and unintentional overdose deaths for each year analyzed along with the corresponding confidence intervals, where applicable.

Figure 1. Measures of Adverse Health Consequences Related to Abuse and Misuse of Prescription Pain Relievers among the U.S. Population Aged 12 and Older, 2003 to 2009.

increased focus on pain management.[25] Officials from a number of agencies noted, however, that while most prescription pain relievers are used as prescribed, a fraction of all prescribed pain relievers are abused and misused.[26] Available data do not allow officials to determine what fraction of prescription pain relievers are abused and misused.

Officials from multiple agencies suggested that adverse health consequences may also be increasing because more individuals who abuse or misuse prescription pain relievers may be abusing or misusing extended-release and long-acting pain reliever formulations, though data from which to draw this conclusion are limited. Because extended-release and long-acting formulations are designed to release their ingredients and relieve pain over an extended period of time, they may have more pain-relieving ingredients in each dose than immediate-release drugs. Prescriptions dispensed for these extended-release and long-acting formulations increased by 56 percent from 2003 to 2009—an even higher rate than the increase for prescription pain relievers overall.[27] FDA officials said that, because of their potency, when extended-release and long-acting drugs are abused and misused, they are more likely to cause harm than when immediate-release pain relievers are abused. For example, an FDA analysis found that extended-release and long-acting pain relievers are more often involved in emergency department visits than immediate-release pain relievers, when adjusted for number of prescriptions.[28] In addition, a 2009 analysis by a panel of experts associated methadone, a long-acting pain reliever, with a high number of deaths compared with other prescription pain relievers, when adjusted for the total number of prescriptions dispensed.[29,30] Officials from most of the agencies we interviewed said that they are most concerned about extended-release and long-acting pain relievers, but they noted that immediate-release pain relievers are also abused and misused. Officials from multiple agencies noted, however, that data on what drug formulations are being abused and misused are limited because most measures of abuse and misuse do not gather information on the particular drug formulation involved in a case of an adverse health consequence or self-reported abuse and misuse.

A second factor that officials from several agencies said likely contributed to the increases in adverse health consequences is that more individuals may be engaging in high-risk behaviors when they abuse or misuse prescription pain relievers, though data on the extent of high-risk behaviors are limited. One high-risk behavior officials pointed to was combining prescription pain relievers with other substances, such as another prescription pain reliever, alcohol, or other drugs. Taken together, the interactions of such substances can lead to increased risk of life-threatening conditions. From 2004 to 2009, the number of emergency department visits that involved combining prescription pain relievers with other substances increased by an estimated 200,000 visits, while the number of emergency department visits involving a prescription pain reliever alone increased by an estimated 88,000 visits.[31] However, officials from several agencies told us that their understanding of how drugs are used in combination is limited by the available data. For example, NSDUH, which reports estimates of abuse and misuse based on a nationwide survey, does not ask survey respondents which substances they use in combination. In addition, NVSS data on unintentional overdose deaths are limited by the amount of detail listed on death certificates. Not all substances involved in a death may be listed on a death certificate, especially when a toxicology report is not used to determine the cause of death. CDC officials said that whether a toxicology report is used to determine the cause of death varies by jurisdiction, and currently, the number of postmortem examinations, which may include toxicology reports, is declining.

Officials from multiple agencies said that another high-risk behavior that may be leading to increased adverse health consequences is inhaling or injecting the drugs, rather than taking them orally as prescribed. From 2003 to 2009, the percentage of admissions to substance abuse treatment facilities where the admitted individual reported usually abusing or misusing prescription pain relievers through inhaling the drugs increased from 9 percent to 16 percent of cases. The percent of admissions where the admitted individual reported using the drugs orally decreased from 72 to 69 percent of cases, while the percent of admissions using the drugs in other ways was stable. NIH has reported that inhaling and injecting drugs is more dangerous than taking them orally as prescribed. Inhaling or injecting the drugs delivers drugs more quickly to the brain and can increase the risk of addiction and overdose.

FEDERAL AGENCIES ARE USING VARIOUS STRATEGIES TO EDUCATE PRESCRIBERS ABOUT ISSUES RELATED TO PRESCRIPTION PAIN RELIEVER ABUSE AND MISUSE

FDA, NIH, and SAMHSA are using a variety of strategies to fill the gaps federal agencies have identified in prescriber education related to treating pain, prescribing opioids appropriately, and identifying substance abuse in their patients, but officials told us that more education is needed. Strategies that these agencies pursued in fiscal year 2011 include developing CME programs, requiring training and certification in order to prescribe certain drugs, organizing physician mentoring networks, and developing curriculum resources for future prescribers.

First, FDA, NIH, and SAMHSA are using voluntary CME programs to educate prescribers about issues related to prescription pain reliever abuse and misuse. CME programs are educational activities which serve to maintain, develop, and increase the knowledge, skills, and professional performance and relationships physicians use to provide services to patients. Many state medical boards require prescribers to complete a certain number of CME credits for license re-registration. FDA is requiring manufacturers to develop a CME or continuing education (CE) course for prescribers as part of a Risk Evaluation and Mitigation Strategy (REMS) for extended-release and long-acting prescription pain relievers.[32,33] While completion of the course, which is expected to be implemented in early 2012, will be voluntary, FDA is requiring manufacturers to propose performance goals for the percentage of prescribers who complete it. NIH is undertaking a different approach to using CME programs to educate prescribers about identification of substance abuse in their patients, reaching out to prescribers at medical conferences across the country. Using a live theater CME format, NIH uses a dramatic reading of a portion of the play *Long Day's Journey into Night* that focuses on a character's morphine addiction, an expert panel reaction, and a facilitated audience discussion to highlight issues like incorporating screening, brief intervention, and referral to treatment into primary care settings. Finally, SAMHSA developed a CME course on prescribing opioids for chronic pain and partners with local host organizations, such as local medical organizations and state agencies, to offer it across the United States. The course is targeted at physicians, dentists, and other prescribers and can be modified to reflect the needs of the local host organization.

Another strategy FDA uses is requiring prescribers of certain prescription pain relievers to be trained and certified in order to prescribe them. As of October 2011, all five marketed transmucosal immediate-release fentanyl products had REMS with prescriber training and certification components due to unique concerns associated with these products.[34] In order to become certified to prescribe these drugs for outpatient use, prescribers must review written materials, successfully complete a knowledge assessment, and register with the manufacturer of the drug by completing a prescriber enrollment form, which includes a commitment to complete a patient-prescriber agreement with each new patient.[35] Prescribers are required to become recertified every 2 years.

A third strategy NIH and SAMHSA are pursuing is providing funding to develop physician clinical support systems, which provide educational resources and free, nationwide mentoring services related to prescribing prescription pain relievers. As of October 2011, two physician clinical support systems had been funded: one to assist practicing physicians interested in implementing substance abuse screening in their practices and one related to the appropriate use of prescription pain relievers for the treatment of chronic pain.[36] Each system links physicians to trained clinical advisors who can provide telephone or e-mail responses to specific questions and offer support using the educational resources.

The final strategy NIH and SAMHSA are using is developing curricula for future prescribers, including medical students and residents, about issues related to prescription pain reliever abuse and misuse. NIDA's Centers of Excellence for Physician Information, located in eight medical schools, are developing curriculum resources—including lectures, faculty workshops, and web modules—to help train medical students and residents to screen, treat, and refer patients with substance use disorders. As of October 2011, the medical schools had developed 10 curriculum resources, 5 of which are specific to prescription drug abuse and misuse. In addition, NIDA is taking the lead on a project with participation from more than 10 institutes and centers within the NIH to establish the NIH Pain Consortium Centers of Excellence in Pain Education. These Centers of Excellence aim to develop curricula that will educate medical students about best practices in the treatment of pain by fiscal year 2014. SAMHSA is also facilitating the development of curricula for training medical residents. Through its Screening, Brief Intervention, Referral and Treatment Medical Residency Program, medical residency programs are developing curricula and clinical training for identifying substance use disorders, including training about issues related to prescription drug abuse and misuse, and incorporating the curricula and clinical training into 16 residency programs.[37] The curriculum resources for these programs are designed to be transferable to medical schools and residency programs nationwide.

Despite various ongoing strategies to educate current and future prescribers about issues related to prescription pain reliever abuse and misuse, officials from each of the federal agencies we spoke with told us that more prescriber education is necessary. ONDCP officials indicated that they—with technical assistance from DEA, FDA, and SAMHSA—are working to develop a legislative proposal to require that all prescribers who request DEA registration to prescribe controlled substances be trained on the appropriate and safe use, proper storage, and disposal of prescription pain relievers as a precondition of registration. Currently, in order to register with DEA to prescribe a controlled substance, prescribers must hold a valid state license.[38] Officials from many of the agencies we spoke with expressed support for mandatory prescriber education, with some noting that this would ensure that all prescribers were starting from the same baseline of knowledge. Officials from one agency expressed support for promoting the education of all prescribers through other means, such as working with state medical boards. Officials from several agencies explained that more prescriber education is necessary because the majority of educational strategies that federal agencies are currently pursuing are voluntary and may not reach the majority of either current or future prescribers. Because training could help prescribers feel more comfortable prescribing these drugs, ONDCP officials also explained that mandatory prescriber education could improve access to prescription pain relievers for patients with a legitimate need for pain relief. Officials from ONDCP also noted that by mandating education for all prescribers, rather than only for those who prescribed extended-release and long-acting prescription pain relievers, they could avoid a possible situation in which some prescribers would be unable to prescribe certain pain relievers because they had chosen not to take the training. Representatives of the American Medical Association told us that they, along with a number of other associations representing prescribers, favored the use of positive incentives—such as a reduction in the $551 fee prescribers pay to DEA when registering to prescribe controlled substances—to encourage prescribers to complete voluntary education about these issues, rather than mandating such education. The American Medical Association representatives noted that the contribution that poor prescribing practices or fraudulent activity on the part of prescribers makes to the supply of prescription pain relievers that are diverted for abuse and misuse is unknown. As a result, they told us that it is unclear whether mandatory prescriber education would have an effect on prescription pain reliever abuse and misuse.

FEDERAL AGENCIES GENERALLY FOLLOWED KEY PRACTICES WHEN DEVELOPING PUBLIC EDUCATION EFFORTS

All federal agencies used almost all of the key practices for developing consumer education efforts, which varied in size, scope, and duration. Agencies also varied in how they used key practices when developing these efforts. All agencies established metrics to monitor the implementation and functional elements of their educational efforts, but only two agencies have established or are planning to establish metrics to assess the impact of their efforts on audiences' knowledge, attitudes, and behavior.

All Agencies Followed Almost All Key Practices; Efforts Varied in Size and Approach

All federal agencies used almost all of the key practices for developing consumer education efforts when developing the efforts that we reviewed to educate the general public about prescription pain reliever abuse and misuse. In fiscal year 2011, five agencies operated nine educational efforts targeted at the general public, ranging from websites to brochures to a museum exhibit (see app. IV for full descriptions of the educational efforts). Our prior work outlines key practices that agencies should engage in when developing public education efforts: define key goals and objectives of the educational effort; analyze the situation, including identifying competing voices or timing considerations; identify stakeholders and clarify their roles; identify resources; research target audiences, including identifying audience characteristics and motivators; develop clear, consistent messages; identify credible messenger(s); design a mix of media, including method and frequency of delivery; and establish metrics to measure success (for further description of these key practices, see app. III).[39] Our review of initiatives to educate the general public about prescription pain reliever abuse and misuse shows that all of the agencies used almost all of these practices when developing their initiatives (see fig. 2). For instance, FDA relied on seven of nine key practices when developing outreach materials for its *Opioid Public Service Announcements*. Other agencies used more key practices when developing their education efforts; ONDCP relied on all nine key practices for developing consumer education efforts when it developed the prescription drug content for the *National Youth Anti-Drug Media Campaign.*

Agency	Education effort	Define goals and objectives	Analyze the situation	Identify stakeholders	Identify resources	Research target audiences	Develop consistent, clear messages	Identify credible messenger(s)	Design media mix	Establish metrics to measure success: Process metrics	Establish metrics to measure success: Outcome metrics
DEA	Just Think Twice[a]	✓	✓	✓	✓	✓	✓	✓	✓	✓	
	Get Smart About Drugs[a]	✓	✓	✓	✓	✓	✓	✓	✓	✓	
	Take Back Initiative[b]	✓	✓	✓	✓	✓	✓	✓	✓	✓	
	Good Medicine, Bad Behavior	✓	✓	✓	✓	✓	✓	✓	✓	✓	
FDA	Opioid Public Service Announcements	✓	✓		✓		✓	✓	✓	✓	
NIH	Heads Up: Real News About Drugs and Your Body[a]	✓	✓	✓	✓	✓	✓	✓	✓	✓	
	NIDA for Teens[a]	✓	✓	✓	✓	✓	✓	✓	✓	✓	✓
ONDCP	National Youth Anti-Drug Media Campaign[a]	✓	✓	✓	✓	✓	✓	✓	✓	✓	✓
SAMHSA	Not Worth The Risk; Even if it's Legal	✓	✓	✓	✓	✓	✓	✓	✓	✓	

Source: GAO analysis of information from DEA, FDA, NIH, ONDCP, and SAMHSA.

[a]Efforts are broader than prescription drugs. We limited our analysis to the prescription drug-related components of these efforts.

[b]According to DEA officials, the primary purpose of the *Take Back Initiative* is to collect and dispose of unwanted and unused prescription drugs. Public education about prescription drug storage and disposal is a secondary goal. We limited our analysis to the public education materials associated with the *Take Back Initiative.*

Figure 2. Agencies' Use of Key Practices for Developing Public Education Efforts.

Agencies varied in how they used the key practices for developing public education efforts. For instance, SAMHSA used the key practice of developing consistent, clear messages by convening Project Advisory Teams composed of external stakeholders and subject matter experts. The teams met several times during the development of two phases of *Not Worth the Risk; Even if it's Legal* and gave input to SAMHSA about effective messaging and distribution channels for the program's target audiences, which include teens, college students, and "student influencers" (e.g, parents, teachers, health care providers). FDA used a different approach for the same key practice of developing consistent, clear messages for its *Opioid Public Service Announcements*—which include information about appropriate use, storage, and disposal of medications—relying on internal discussions between staff in its Office of Communications and the Office of New Drugs.

Although all agencies used many of the same key practices to develop their educational efforts, the resulting initiatives are different in terms of size, scope, and duration, and agencies dedicated varying amounts of resources to developing their efforts. For instance, NIH's *Heads Up: Real News About Drugs and Your Body* provides classroom materials— including magazine articles, student worksheets, and lesson plans—to students and teachers about a range of topics related to drug abuse and misuse, including but not limited to prescription drugs, and has done so each school year since 2002. By contrast, DEA began collecting and disposing of unused prescription drugs through its *Take Back Initiative* in 2010.[40] The agency developed outreach materials to raise awareness of the event and the materials—including brochures and bill-boards—are specific to prescription drugs. There is also significant variation in terms of the resources different agencies used for program development. For instance, the budget for the *National Youth Anti-Drug Media Campaign* in fiscal year 2011 was approximately $35 million, whereas *Not Worth the Risk; Even if it's Legal* cost about $80,000 for the last phase of the brochure series.[41] Many programs we reviewed cost less than $150,000 for program development and dissemination in a fiscal year.

All Agencies Followed the Key Practice of Establishing Process Metrics but Most Did Not Assess Program Outcomes

While all agencies established metrics to monitor the implementation and functional elements of their educational initiatives, only two agencies have established or planned to establish metrics to assess the impact of their initiatives on audiences' knowledge, attitudes, and behavior with regard to prescription pain reliever abuse and misuse. The former, known as process metrics, monitor the operational elements of educational efforts, such as the quantity or volume of outreach efforts. The latter, known as outcome metrics, are used to assess the impact of the initiative on the desired health or behavior outcome. Our prior work and other guides for developing consumer education efforts note that establishing both process and outcome metrics are critical elements of program development.[42]

All federal agencies followed the key practice of establishing process metrics for the public education efforts we reviewed. For instance, DEA tracks the amount of activity and use across the different features and content pages on its websites, *Just Think Twice and Get Smart About Drugs*, including the most popular search terms and amount of time spent on the components of the websites. DEA also monitors the number of visitors to its museum exhibit about prescription drug abuse and misuse, *Good Medicine, Bad Behavior*, and records the number of group visits by category (e.g., schools, universities, or senior citizens).

ONDCP and NIH were the only agencies that followed the key practice of establishing outcome metrics for their education efforts. ONDCP measures outcomes from its *National Youth Anti-Drug Media Campaign* (the Campaign) on a weekly basis through ongoing tracking studies. The tracking studies survey 100 teens each week about awareness of the Campaign and their attitudes, beliefs, and intentions regarding drug use, including where and how teens interact with the Campaign's website, and attitudes after interacting with the website.[43] ONDCP also awarded a contract to evaluate the Campaign's contribution to preventing drug abuse among young people in the United States, in particular by assessing the Campaign's impact on knowledge, attitudes, beliefs, and behavioral intention about drug use.[44] However, ONDCP indicated that, as of September 2011, the contract was being terminated because the Campaign has not been funded for fiscal year 2012. NIH plans to evaluate outcomes for its *NIDA for Teens* website by surveying students and teachers about students' knowledge acquisition and attitude change after exposure to *NIDA for Teens*, as well as teachers' opinions on the utility of the website. Although officials from agencies that did not establish outcome metrics told us that they recognize the importance of evaluating public education efforts, they cited challenges measuring the impact of such efforts and lack of financial resources as reasons for not assessing program outcomes. For instance, one official explained that an outcome evaluation for his agency's drug education program would cost more than developing and implementing the program itself.

Beyond the key practices for developing public education efforts, our prior work notes that using existing evidence to inform public health communications, such as research on teen messaging or evaluations of related efforts, can also be helpful in analyzing the effectiveness of educational efforts in addition to establishing outcome metrics.[45] When developing their public education efforts, agencies incorporated evidence-based strategies when possible, but limited evidence exists about how to successfully educate the public about prescription pain reliever abuse and misuse.

For instance, research shows that teens may mistakenly believe that prescription pain relievers are safer than illicit drugs. As a result, officials from several agencies told us that they seek to dispel this misperception in their educational efforts. In addition, NSDUH data also indicate that most people who abuse or misuse prescription pain relievers get the drugs from a friend or family member. Thus, DEA officials told us that they have sought to educate the public about proper drug storage and disposal in order to limit the amount of drugs that are available to be diverted from medicine cabinets for abuse and misuse.

However, officials from multiple agencies explained that because there are distinct challenges when designing educational efforts about prescription pain reliever abuse and misuse compared to other drug prevention efforts, more research is needed in order to understand how to craft effective messages, particularly for teens. Officials said that education about prescription pain reliever abuse and misuse requires a more nuanced approach because there are legitimate medical uses for these products.

In addition, officials from several agencies noted that educational efforts should avoid inadvertently alerting people to the possibility of using these drugs to get high. The motivations for abusing and misusing prescription drugs can also be different than the motivations for using illicit drugs, such as self-medicating for pain relief, and understanding how to effectively target the variety of reasons people abuse and misuse prescription drugs is another area that requires more research, according to agency officials. The Surgeon General, with support from other federal agencies, is currently developing a Call to Action on youth prescription drug abuse that will discuss available evidence to support prevention strategies, including educational efforts.[46] An official from the Office of the Surgeon General told us that the Call to Action, which is anticipated for release in February 2012, will also identify gaps in existing research related to youth prescription drug abuse prevention strategies and call for further research to be conducted to fill these gaps.

Federal Agencies Have Begun Coordinating Similar Public and Prescriber Education Efforts, but Have Missed Opportunities to Share Resources

There are several similarities among agencies' efforts, target audiences, and mediums across the nine public education initiatives and nine prescriber education programs we identified. Officials said that these similarities in public education efforts are beneficial in addressing prescription drug abuse and misuse because having multiple, reinforcing messages about the same subject is valuable in public health communications and because federal agencies provide slightly different perspectives on the issues surrounding prescription drug abuse and misuse. Likewise, the prescriber education programs we identified, though similar, are different in content and focus. Although these similar programs have the potential to be duplicative if not effectively coordinated, federal agencies have recently begun to coordinate their educational efforts. Nevertheless, federal agencies have missed opportunities to pool resources—a key practice for effective coordination—among similar education efforts, which may have resulted in lost opportunities to obtain additional benefits through coordination.

Federal Agencies Operate Similar Public and Prescriber Education Programs

Among all nine federal initiatives to educate the general public about prescription pain reliever abuse and misuse that we reviewed, there are several instances of agencies engaging in similar efforts (see table 1). Officials told us that it is beneficial to have similar education efforts about prescription pain reliever abuse and misuse because of the complex nature of this problem and the fact that agencies provide different but reinforcing messages about the issue.

For example, three initiatives—*Just Think Twice*, *NIDA for Teens*, and the *National Youth Anti-Drug Media Campaign*—use the same medium to target teens with similar messages about prescription drug abuse and misuse. These efforts provide web-based information and interactive features to educate teens about prescription drug abuse and misuse. (See fig. 3 and fig. 4 for examples of web-based efforts to educate teens about prescription drug abuse and misuse.) Officials working on these efforts noted that they chose to focus on teens because drug abuse typically starts during teen years. NIH officials told us that prescription and over-the-counter medications account for most of the drugs commonly abused by 12th graders as well, after alcohol, tobacco, and marijuana. Teens are also more vulnerable to the negative effects of drug use since their brains are still developing.

Table 1. Public Education Efforts about Prescription Pain Reliever Abuse and Misuse

Primary target audience	Agency	Program	Medium
Teens	DEA	Good Medicine, Bad Behavior	Museum exhibit
		Just Think Twice[a]	Website
	NIH	Heads Up: Real News About Drugs and Your Body[a]	Classroom materials
		NIDA for Teens[a]	Website
	ONDCP	National Youth Anti-Drug Media Campaign[a]	Website
	SAMHSA	Not Worth the Risk; Even if it's Legal	Brochures and posters
Parents	DEA	Get Smart About Drugs[a]	Website
	ONDCP	National Youth Anti-Drug Media Campaign[a]	Website
	SAMHSA	Not Worth the Risk; Even if it's Legal	Brochures and posters
College students	SAMHSA	Not Worth the Risk; Even if it's Legal	Brochures and posters
Teachers	NIH	Heads Up: Real News About Drugs and Your Body[a]	Classroom materials
	SAMHSA	Not Worth the Risk; Even if it's Legal	Brochures and posters
Public	DEA	Take Back Initiative	Posters, brochures, advertisements
	FDA	Opioid Public Service Announcements	Audio, slides

Source: GAO analysis of information from NIH, SAMHSA, FDA, DEA, and ONDCP.

Notes: See app. IV for detailed program descriptions.

[a] Efforts are broader than prescription drugs. We limited our analysis to the prescription drug-related components of these efforts.

There are also two initiatives—DEA's *Get Smart About Drugs* and ONDCP's *National Youth Anti-Drug Media Campaign*—that use the same medium to target parents with similar messages about prescription drug abuse and misuse.

For instance, both use websites that have interactive features that show parents where teens commonly access prescription drugs in the home. Both sites also include tips for parents about how to talk to teens about drugs and about how to identify signs of abuse.

ONDCP's Above the Influence website | **NIH's Teen Drug Abuse website**

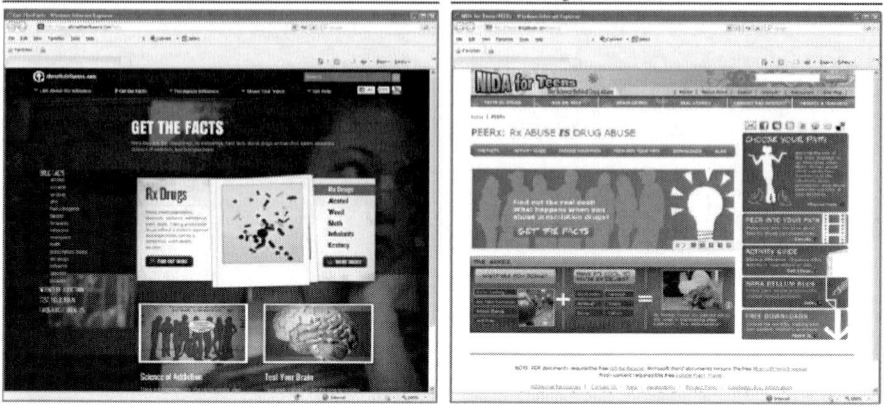

The prescription drug fact page on ONDCP's teen website for the National Youth Anti-Drug Media Campaign (known as Above the Influence).

To view this web page, scan this QR code with your smartphone. Need a QR code reader? Download one for free, then point your phone's camera here.
(URL valid as of report printing date.)

The home page for PEERx, the prescription drug website within NIDA for Teens.

To view this web page, scan this QR code with your smartphone. Need a QR code reader? Download one for free, then point your phone's camera here.
(URL valid as of report printing date.)

Source: ONDCP, NIH, GAO.
Figure 3. ONDCP and NIH Teen Websites.

Officials acknowledged these instances of similar goals and similar strategies to reach the same audience among educational efforts. However, officials said that these similarities are beneficial in addressing prescription drug abuse and misuse.

Officials from NIH, FDA, DEA, and ONDCP noted that having multiple, reinforcing messages about the same subject is valuable in public health communications, particularly about an issue as complex as prescription drug abuse and misuse. The National Council on Patient Information and Education also told us that repetition and frequent delivery of information supports message reinforcement. Second, federal agencies have their own constituencies and each approaches prescription drug abuse and misuse from a slightly different perspective. For instance, NIDA for Teens provides a science-based perspective and includes information about how prescription drugs affect the brain. Specifically, the "Mind Over Matter" series on the NIDA for Teens website explains how prescription drugs mimic neurotransmitters to alter the brain's chemistry.

DEA's Just Think Twice, on the other hand, pro-vides more information about the legal consequences of abusing drugs, such as losing federal student loans, and the culture of drug abuse, including images of drugs and true stories of youth overdose deaths. NIH officials told us that both perspectives are important as some members of the public may go to NIH's NIDA for information about these issues, while others may go to DEA.

DEA's Just Think Twice website

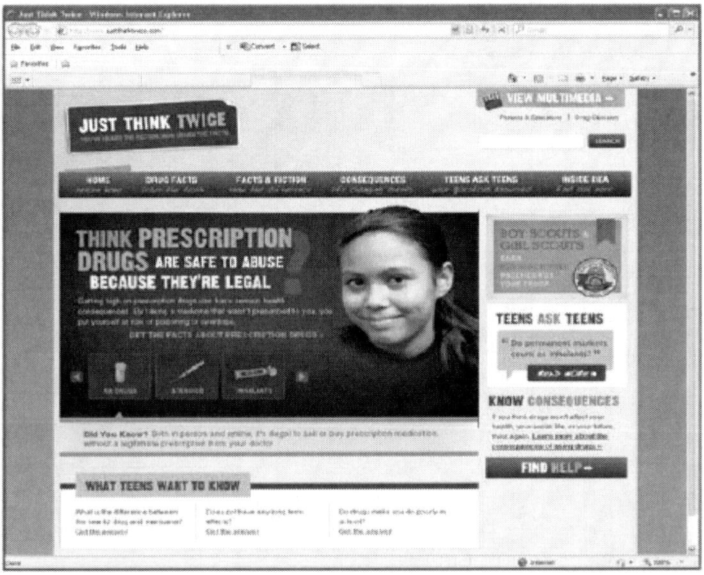

The home page for DEA's teen education website, Just Think Twice, which provides information about a range of abused drugs, including prescription drugs.

To view this web page, scan this QR code with your smartphone. Need a QR code reader? Download one for free, then point your phone's camera here. (URL valid as of report printing date.)

Source: DEA, GAO.
Figure 4. DEA Teen Website.

Officials also said that they cross-reference each other's information when appropriate. For instance, ONDCP links to publications from NIH's NIDA on one of the *National Youth Anti-Drug Media Campaign* websites.

In addition to the similarities among the nine targeted educational efforts we reviewed, agencies are engaged in additional efforts outside the scope of our review which, taken together, may present areas of potential duplication.[47] These additional efforts include posting materials from retired initiatives online, planning future efforts, and providing factual information about prescription pain relievers. For instance, FDA and SAMHSA have brochures and posters for teens and the elderly with messages about prescription pain reliever abuse and misuse that are no longer actively disseminated, but are still available on their websites. HRSA and, contingent on available resources, DEA are also planning to launch new or update existing educational initiatives in the next fiscal year, targeted at the elderly and parents, respectively.

Table 2. Efforts to Educate Prescribers about Issues Related to Prescription Pain Reliever Abuse and Misuse

Target audience	Program (Agency)	Medium	Content of training
Current prescribers	Extended-release and long-acting opioid REMS (FDA)	CME/CE course	Appropriate prescribing[a]
	Addiction Performance Project (NIH)[b]	CME course	Screening, brief intervention, and referral to treatment[c]
	Prescribing Opioids for Chronic Pain (SAMHSA)	CME course	Appropriate prescribing
	Transmucosal immediate-release fentanyl REMS (FDA)	Written materials	Appropriate prescribing
	Physician Clinical Support System – Primary Care (NIH)[b]	Written materials, screening tools, mentoring	Screening, brief intervention, and referral to treatment
	Prescriber's Clinical Support System for the Appropriate Use of Opioids in the Treatment of Pain and Opioid-related Addiction (SAMHSA)	Written materials, mentoring, webinars	Appropriate prescribing[a]
Future prescribers	NIDA Centers of Excellence for Physician Information (NIH)[b]	Curricular resources, including lectures, case studies, and web-based training	Appropriate prescribing; screening,brief intervention, and referral to treatment
	NIH Pain Consortium Centers of Excellence in Pain Education (NIH)	Curricular resources	Treating pain[a]
	Screening, Brief Intervention, Referral and Treatment Medical Residency Program (SAMHSA)[b]	Curricular resources, including lectures, web-based training, and role plays, and clinical training, including practice with simulated patients	Screening, brief intervention, and referral to treatment

Source: GAO.

Notes: The Addiction Performance Project, Physician Clinical Support System—Primary Care, and Centers of Excellence for Physician Information are all part of the NIDAMED physician outreach initiative, designed to provide tools and resources to assist physicians in addressing substance abuse (including prescription drug abuse) in their practices. Another component of this initiative is NIH's Drug Use Screening Tool, a web-based interactive screening tool for use in primary care practices that specifically captures information on patient prescription drug abuse.

[a]Content is anticipated as materials have not yet been developed.

[b]Programs are broader than prescription drugs. We limited our analysis to the prescription drug-related components of these programs.

[c]According to NIH officials, the primary goal of the Addiction Performance Project is to help break down the stigma associated with addiction. Educating prescribers about screening, brief intervention, and referral to treatment is a secondary goal.

ONDCP is also planning to work with agencies and external stakeholders to develop and implement national public education campaigns on prescription drug abuse and misuse and drug storage and disposal, by April 2013. ONDCP officials told us that, as of October 2011, they were still considering various options and working to identify resources for these campaigns. Finally, three federal agencies have prescription drug fact pages on their main websites and FDA oversees the dissemination of drug information to patients through tools such as medication guides that are provided with some prescription drugs. Given the number of agencies involved in educating the public about prescription pain reliever abuse and misuse and the number of efforts currently under way, these additional efforts represent areas where there may be the potential for duplicative programming, if such efforts are not effectively coordinated.

There are also similar target audiences and mediums among the nine prescriber education programs we identified, although the content and focus of these programs is different (see table 2). For example, two CME courses, SAMHSA's Prescribing Opioids for Chronic Pain course and FDA's requirement for prescriber education through its extended-release and long-acting opioid REMS, are both targeted at current prescribers. Though these courses have some similar content about patient selection and monitoring, FDA officials noted that prescriber education through REMS will focus on extended-release and long-acting products, whereas the SAMHSA course includes information on both extended-release and immediate-release pain relievers. They also noted that the SAMHSA course is more focused on addiction and treatment than the REMS materials will be. As a result, prescribers are being educated about the full range of issues related to prescription pain reliever abuse and misuse, including treating pain, appropriate prescribing, and recognizing substance abuse in their patients.

Federal Agencies Coordinate Their Educational Efforts through Three Main Mechanisms and Have Increasingly Relied on Key Practices for Coordination

Federal agencies use three main mechanisms—two mechanisms that are overseen by ONDCP, the National Drug Control Strategy and the Prescription Drug Abuse Prevention Plan, and one mechanism within HHS, the HHS Behavioral Health Coordinating Committee's Subcommittee on Prescription Drug Abuse—to coordinate their educational efforts. The agencies have also begun using key practices for coordination that we have identified in prior work on practices that help enhance and sustain collaboration.[48] ONDCP releases the National Drug Control Strategy (the Strategy) on an annual basis and it outlines the administration's goals and priorities for reducing the rate of drug abuse and misuse and the associated consequences. The Strategy, which outlines drug control policies and programs for illicit and prescription drugs, serves as a coordination mechanism for drug control agencies and incorporates several key practices for interagency collaboration. For instance, the Strategy defines and articulates a common outcome by establishing the administration's goals for reducing drug abuse and misuse. The Strategy also provides a means for agencies to agree on roles and responsibilities by listing specific actions for agencies to take, including identifying lead and partnering agencies for each action item. For example, "Enhance Healthcare Providers' Skills in Screening and Brief Intervention" is an action item in the 2010 Strategy and it specifies that SAMHSA is the lead agency, with NIH's NIDA, HRSA, and the Indian Health Service listed as partnering agencies. Finally, the Strategy provides a means to monitor, evaluate, and report on results for collaborative efforts. Agencies developed objectives and 1- and 2-year milestones for the action items in the 2010 Strategy and they submit regular progress reports to ONDCP.

The Prescription Drug Abuse Prevention Plan (the Plan) was recently released by ONDCP and complements the Strategy by outlining the administration's approach to addressing prescription drug abuse and misuse, in particular. As a result, it serves as a second interagency coordination mechanism for agencies addressing prescription drug abuse and also reflects the key practices for collaboration that we previously identified. The Plan establishes mutually reinforcing or joint strategies by identifying four priority areas for federal efforts to reduce prescription drug abuse and misuse—education, monitoring, proper disposal, and enforcement—and it aligns agencies' activities around these four areas. For instance, the Plan calls for federal agencies and private stakeholders to work together to develop evidence-based public education campaigns about appropriate use, secure storage, disposal, and abuse of prescription drugs. Like the Strategy, the Plan also provides a means to monitor, evaluate, and report on results. ONDCP asked agencies to submit implementation plans with objectives and 1- and 2-year milestones and to provide progress reports on a quarterly basis. The Plan also calls for the establishment of a Federal Council on Prescription Drug Abuse to coordinate implementation of the Plan.

Finally, the HHS Behavioral Health Coordinating Committee's Subcommittee on Prescription Drug Abuse provides a third coordination mechanism for HHS agencies and demonstrates use of the key practices for collaboration as well. For instance, the Subcommittee defines a common outcome for HHS agencies by identifying five goals related to prescription drug abuse and organizing its activities around these goals.[49] The Subcommittee also provides a means to monitor and report on progress to HHS leadership. Agency officials report on their activities related to prescription drug abuse and misuse to the Subcommittee co-chairs, who then provide updates to HHS leadership.

Agencies have begun using these coordination mechanisms, or augmenting existing coordination efforts, within recent years. Beginning in 2009, ONDCP began using a more collaborative process for developing the Strategy, convening a Demand Reduction Interagency Working Group. The working group brought together subject experts from drug control agencies to provide input on the development of the Strategy and DEA, FDA, HRSA, NIH, and SAMHSA all participated. Officials from multiple agencies indicated that this process was more interactive than in years past. The 2010 Strategy also utilized a new approach by outlining specific action items and developing a system to monitor agency progress toward objectives. ONDCP also released the Plan in April 2011 and agency officials described the process for developing the Plan as collaborative. One official described the amount of brainstorming between ONDCP and agencies in order to develop the Plan as "unprecedented." Finally, the Subcommittee on Prescription Drug Abuse was formed in the summer of 2010. Officials explained that the Subcommittee provides a more regular and formal means of coordination, whereas prior efforts to coordinate within HHS were more irregular and informal. For instance, the Subcommittee helped institutionalize relationships among officials who work on prescription drug abuse and misuse across HHS. Officials noted that although they were previously aware of subject experts at other agencies, they now work together on related tasks through the Subcommittee and therefore have formal working relationships which they can draw on to work through issues. Subcommittee members added that they use their meetings to share programming information. For instance, prior to convening the Subcommittee, NIH officials told us that they were not fully aware of all of the prescriber education efforts across HHS agencies. Now, officials have created a group through the Subcommittee to catalogue related prescriber education programs.

While officials from each agency we spoke with said that these coordination mechanisms were working well, ONDCP and other agency officials indicated that they were aware of the potential for creating too many coordinating bodies. Though the Strategy's Demand Reduction Interagency Working Group, the Plan's new Federal Council on Prescription Drug Abuse, and the HHS Subcommittee on Prescription Drug Abuse may have membership from many of the same agencies, officials said that they felt that they had not reached the point of too much coordination, noting that current coordination efforts were effective in terms of facilitating information sharing and avoiding overlapping programming among agencies.

Federal Agencies Have Missed Opportunities to Leverage Resources among Efforts with Similar Goals

Although agencies have increased their coordination efforts in recent years, they have missed opportunities to leverage resources—a key practice for effective coordination—among similar education efforts targeting teens, which may have resulted in lost opportunities to obtain additional benefits through coordination. At least four teen initiatives— *Just Think Twice*, *NIDA for Teens*, the *National Youth Anti-Drug Media Campaign*, and *Not Worth the Risk*; *Even if it's Legal*—have obtained feedback from teens and other stakeholders about the features of and messages for educational efforts about prescription drug abuse and misuse that was not shared. For instance, NIH formed a Teen Advisory Group to pretest their messages and also seeks input from local high school students, including groups such as Students Against Destructive Decisions. These focus groups revealed information that could be useful to other teen education efforts, addressing topics such as web and materials design, video content, language and terminology, and messaging. For instance, one focus group revealed that trying to imitate the layout of social networking sites (e.g., MySpace or Facebook) did not make sites more appealing to teen users.

DEA, ONDCP, and SAMHSA also get feedback on their teen education efforts. DEA gets feedback from the Drug Abuse Resistance Education—D.A.R.E.—Youth Advisory Board on content for *Just Think Twice* and also gets feedback from DEA field staff who give presentations to teens about drug abuse. DEA officials told us that the feedback on the website that they received from field staff often varies depending on the part of the country in which the field staff give presentations in schools, with field staff in San Diego reporting different successful approaches than those in Miami. ONDCP also pretests content and features with teens. One lesson derived from ONDCP's pretesting efforts is that teens liked the option to view content posted by their peers on the website, such as photos or stories. Finally, SAMHSA gets input from professional and student groups through its Project Advisory Team for *Not Worth the Risk*; *Even if it's Legal.* For instance, the Project Advisory Team advised SAMHSA on a number of issues related to addressing prescription drug abuse and misuse among teens, including the importance of acknowledging and validating common stressors teens face in order to establish credibility and to create an opportunity to address alternative coping skills.

While each of these agencies obtained feedback on the messages for and features of similar initiatives, agencies did not share the results of their feedback sessions or pretesting efforts with officials from other agencies who work on similar programs. Officials said they did not share the feedback they received for two reasons. First, NIH, DEA, and SAMHSA officials said that they were never asked to do so by other agencies with similar education efforts. Second, ONDCP officials said that they felt that the results of their pretesting would not be useful for other educational efforts. Nonetheless, one official acknowledged that sharing findings from pretesting efforts and other feedback sessions could have been useful when developing the content and messages for their educational effort.

NIH officials said that there are two coordination mechanisms through which they could share information among agencies involved with educational efforts in the future. In addition to its Subcommittee on Prescription Drug Abuse, the HHS Behavioral Health Coordinating Committee also has a Communications Subcommittee and NIH officials said that they can use the Communications Subcommittee to share information about the development of educational efforts among HHS agencies. NIH officials said that they also have the opportunity to share information with agencies outside of HHS through weekly phone calls that ONDCP facilitates with communications staff from DEA, NIH, ONDCP, and SAMHSA, among other agencies.

Conclusions

Abuse and misuse of prescription pain relievers is a large and growing public health problem in the United States. Although DEA, FDA, NIH, ONDCP, and SAMHSA are engaged in multiple efforts to educate the public about prescription pain reliever abuse and misuse, there is limited evidence about how to craft effective messages about this issue. The agencies agree that education about prescription drug abuse and misuse requires a different approach than other drug prevention efforts, but there is a lack of proven strategies and messages on which agencies can model their own educational efforts to ensure that such efforts will have the desired outcome.

In the absence of a strong evidence base, establishing outcome metrics is an especially important key practice to incorporate into the development of educational efforts because outcome metrics provide feedback on the effectiveness of agencies' efforts at preventing prescription pain reliever abuse and misuse. However, seven of the nine public education efforts that we reviewed did not assess program outcomes. This leaves federal agencies with limited knowledge as to whether such efforts are effective.

Given these challenges, there is much to be gained from continued and robust coordination among similar education efforts about prescription pain reliever abuse and misuse. In its role as a coordinating body for federal drug control efforts, ONDCP is uniquely situated to ensure that federal educational efforts are not duplicative and are effectively coordinated. DEA, NIH, SAMHSA, and ONDCP operate similar educational initiatives—including three websites and a brochure series— targeting teens. While agency officials told us that the similar educational efforts we reviewed are reinforcing, it is important that agencies continue to coordinate their efforts as additional planned educational efforts are implemented in order to avoid duplicative programming.

Although agencies involved in educating the public have recently increased their coordination efforts, they have missed opportunities to share the results of teen and stakeholder feedback among similar efforts—a key practice for effective coordination. In developing their educational efforts, DEA, NIH, ONDCP, and SAMHSA obtained feedback from their target audience and other stakeholders that could be useful for other agencies to consider in relation to their own efforts. Although each educational effort has unique features, comments from focus group participants and other stakeholders could produce lessons that other agencies could have drawn on if summaries of those comments had been made available to other agencies to review.

As additional public education efforts are developed agencies will need to leverage resources, including sharing lessons learned from the development and implementation of existing educational efforts, to ensure that they make the best use of limited resources.

RECOMMENDATIONS FOR EXECUTIVE ACTION

In order to ensure that federal efforts to prevent the abuse and misuse of prescription pain relievers are an effective and efficient use of limited government resources, we recommend that the Director of ONDCP take the following three actions:

- Establish outcome metrics and identify resources for conducting outcome evaluations for the national education campaigns about prescription drug abuse and safe storage and disposal proposed in the Prescription Drug Abuse Prevention Plan.
- Develop and implement a plan to evaluate outcomes from the proposed national education campaigns.
- Ensure that federal agencies undertaking similar educational efforts leverage available resources and use coordination mechanisms to share information on the development of their efforts.

AGENCY COMMENTS AND OUR EVALUATION

We provided a draft of this report to ONDCP, the Department of Justice, and HHS for their review and comment. In written comments, ONDCP did not explicitly agree or disagree with our recommendations, but noted that it will continue to work for improved coordination of prescription drug abuse educational efforts and evaluation of outcomes. ONDCP also stated that the prescription drug abuse educational efforts that we reviewed target different populations and address different messages, and suggested that we explain the differences among these efforts in our report.

We revised our report to include an additional reference to our detailed descriptions of the various educational efforts we reviewed, which explain the scope, target audiences, and mediums used among the educational efforts. We also included additional information about the size and scope of ONDCP's *National Youth Anti-Drug Media Campaign*. ONDCP, DEA, and HHS also provided technical comments, which we have incorporated as appropriate.

Marcia Crosse
Director,
Health Care

APPENDIX I: ABUSE-DETERRENT FORMULATIONS OF PRESCRIPTION PAIN RELIEVERS

In order to help address the abuse and misuse of prescription pain relievers, drug manufacturers are developing formulations of these drugs that are specifically designed to deter abuse.[1] We are presenting information on different types of abuse-deterrent formulations of prescription pain relievers, whether they are being used in fiscal year 2011, and challenges related to these products. This appendix is based on our review of scientific literature and Food and Drug Administration (FDA) and manufacturer documents, as well as interviews with FDA officials and representatives of Purdue Pharma L.P., the manufacturer of OxyContin.

Manufacturers of prescription pain relievers have long sought to achieve a balance between creating drugs that are effective for therapeutic use while minimizing their potential for abuse. The scientific articles noted that, in general, abusers seek out drugs that can be smoked, snorted, or taken intravenously, thus providing a more rapid onset of the effects of the drug. Therefore, some manufacturers of prescription pain relievers have focused on making their products tamper resistant, so that the physical or chemical makeup or delivery system of the drug cannot be altered, with the goal of preventing users from accessing and abusing the active ingredient.

Types of Abuse-Deterrent Formulations

There are five different types of abuse-deterrent formulations manufacturers have developed to reduce tampering and abuse of their products, though some drugs may incorporate multiple types. Some of these abuse-deterrent formulations are already being utilized in prescription pain relievers, others are being incorporated into pain relievers that are in the process of being developed, and others have been used in other types of products, but not prescription pain relievers. In general, the different classifications include:[2]

- Physical/Chemical Barriers – Such barriers impart physical or chemical properties to a drug so that it resists manipulation via chewing, grinding, and mixing with alcohol or other common solvents, thus making extraction of the active ingredient difficult. A reformulated version of the prescription pain reliever OxyContin that is currently marketed uses this type of barrier to deter abuse.

- Agonist/Antagonist Combinations – Combinations of agonists and antagonists, which mitigate, block, or reverse the effect of the agonist (the opioid), if manipulated. Two prescription pain relievers that were marketed in fiscal year 2011 use this barrier to deter abuse: Talwin Nx and Embeda (see sidebar).[3]
- Aversion – A combination of substances designed to produce an unpleasant effect if a tampered form is ingested or a higher dosage than directed is used. For example, one formulation designed in the past added niacin to a prescription pain reliever to dissuade abusers because, in high doses, niacin causes headache, sweating, chills, flushing, and general discomfort. While at least one manufacturer has designed prescription pain relievers using the aversion method of abuse-deterrence in the past, FDA officials told us that no such prescription pain relievers are currently marketed.[4]

Example of an Abuse-Deterrent Formulation: Embeda

Embeda is a prescription pain reliever that was designed from inception to be abuse-deterrent. Embeda employs an agonist-antagonist combination in which the antagonist—a substance that counteracts the opioid (in this case, naltrexone)—is embedded within the center of the active ingredient, or agonist (in this case, morphine).

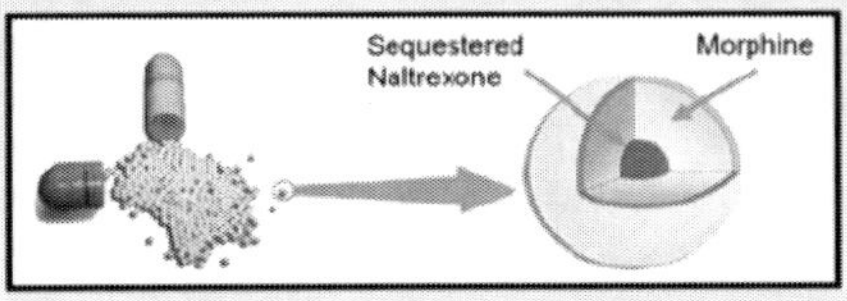

Source: Alpharma Pharmaceuticals, LLC, a subsidiary of Pfizer.

When administered orally, as prescribed, the naltrexone remains pharmacologically inert and the morphine provides pain relief for up to 24 hours. If the capsule is chewed, crushed or dissolved, the naltrexone is activated, inhibiting the psychoactive effect of the morphine and thus making it less attractive to abusers.

Source: GAO and Alpharma Pharmaceuticals, LLC.

- Delivery System – The method of delivery or drug release design can be used as an abuse deterrent. For example, a depot injection—an injection that releases its active ingredient over a sustained period—or subcutaneous implant can be more difficult to tamper with. FDA officials told us that they were not aware of any prescription pain relievers currently marketed that were designed to be abuse-deterrent by way of a delivery system.
- Prodrug – Prodrug compounds must undergo biotransformation to activate the active ingredients. For example, they may be formulated so that they are only activated if they are metabolized in the digestive system, so that the drug will not be activated if, for example, it is taken intravenously. FDA officials told us that they were not aware of any prescription pain relievers currently marketed that were designed to be abuse-deterrent by way of a prodrug design.

Challenges Related to Abuse-Deterrent Prescription Pain Relievers

Manufacturers face a number of challenges related to abuse-deterrent formulations of prescription pain relievers. First, there are technical challenges in developing formulations of prescription pain relievers that deter abuse, but still have the intended effect of providing pain relief. For example, it took Purdue Pharma L.P. approximately 9 years to develop a reformulated version of OxyContin that both effectively provided pain relief and displayed abuse-deterrent properties. Another challenge for manufacturers relates to the extent to which they will be allowed to market their new products as reducing or deterring abuse. FDA officials told us that until postmarketing studies demonstrate a product's effectiveness in reducing abuse in the general population, manufacturers cannot market their products accordingly, but they are allowed to make marketing claims based on the product's abuse-deterrent features as demonstrated in clinical trials. For example, Embeda's label includes information on the results of clinical trails testing its abuse-deterrent features, but also states that the abuse-deterrent characteristics of the product "have not been shown to reduce the abuse liability of Embeda."

Finally, a manufacturer indicated that insurers may be reluctant to provide coverage for abuse-deterrent formulations of drugs when less expensive, non-deterrent alternatives are available and that this could minimize their usage and ultimately, their impact on abuse in the general population.

Example of an Abuse-Deterrent Formulation: OxyContin

OxyContin is a prescription pain reliever that was reformulated to be abuse deterrent. The extended-release mechanism of the original formulation of OxyContin could be overcome by crushing the tablet to release a large amount of oxycodone. Purdue Pharma L.P. reformulated OxyContin to use physical/chemical barriers to deter abuse by mixing the active ingredient—oxycodone—with polyethylene oxide, increasing the hardness of the tablet and rendering it more difficult to crush.

Source: Purdue Pharma L.P.

If the tablet is successfully physically altered through crushing and mixing with a liquid, the result is a viscous gel that is difficult to take up in a syringe.

Source: Purdue Pharma L.P.

Note: According to the manufacturer, the reformulated OxyContin on the right cannot be drawn up into a syringe.

FDA officials told us that only limited, preliminary data about the impact of the reformulated OxyContin on abuse are available (the reformulated OxyContin has only been in widespread use since late 2010). These preliminary data have been promising, but officials were uncertain as to whether any decreases in OxyContin abuse would hold over the long term.

Source: GAO and Purdue Pharma L.P.

FDA faces a number of challenges related to approving and assessing the safety and effectiveness of abuse-deterrent formulations of prescription pain relievers. According to FDA officials, one of these challenges is balancing the abuse-deterrent properties of a drug with its safety in the general patient population. Another challenge for FDA is developing standards and methods for determining if the products are, in fact, abuse deterrent. FDA officials told us that the agency is currently developing guidance for manufacturers on the development of abuse-deterrent formulations and on the postmarket assessment of their performance. However, officials told us that standard guidance is difficult to develop because potential types of abuse-deterrent formulations are so varied that the criteria used to evaluate one drug may not be applicable for another.

FDA indicated that it requires manufacturers of prescription pain relievers that want to make abuse-deterrent claims about their products to conduct postmarket epidemiological studies to assess the effectiveness of their drugs in deterring abuse in the general population. However, in developing methods for assessing the effectiveness of a particular drug on deterring abuse, FDA officials told us that they, like manufacturers, are challenged by limitations in available data. FDA officials said that consistent and clear definitions of abuse across data sources are lacking and that most data sources with information on prescription pain reliever abuse do not distinguish between products from different manufacturers, which can make it difficult to assess the effectiveness of a specific drug in deterring abuse.

For example, data sources that measure abuse and its consequences may not distinguish between OxyContin and other drugs that contain oxycodone. Further, FDA is challenged in determining what degree of decrease in some measurable outcomes of abuse would be sufficient to label a drug as being able to reduce actual abuse.

Finally, there are inherent challenges related to abuse-deterrent formulations of prescription pain relievers and their overall impact on abuse. First, a drug that deters one type of abuse might not necessarily deter another type of abuse. For example, the new formulation of OxyContin is designed to deter abuse via injection or snorting (see sidebar), but is not a deterrent for those who abuse the product via oral ingestion of whole tablets. A related challenge is that while technology may deter the abuse of one particular prescription pain reliever, an abuser may instead seek another prescription pain reliever (either a different formulation of the same pain reliever or a different pain reliever altogether) that is not designed to be abuse deterrent. An abuser may even seek out another opioid, such as heroin.

APPENDIX II: DEA QUOTAS FOR CONTROLLED SUBSTANCES

As part of its responsibilities related to enforcing the Controlled Substances Act, the Drug Enforcement Administration (DEA) sets limits, called quotas, on the quantity of schedule I and II controlled substances that may be produced in the United States in any given calendar year.[1] Quotas are a component of the closed system of distribution that exists under the Controlled Substances Act. In this appendix, we present an overview of the closed system, as well as information on the three types of quotas: aggregate production quotas (APQ), bulk manufacturing quotas, and procurement quotas. The information in this appendix is based on our review of DEA documents and interviews with DEA officials.

Closed Distribution System

Under the Controlled Substances Act, DEA maintains a closed system requiring any person who manufactures, dispenses, imports, exports, or conducts research with controlled substances to register with DEA (unless exempt),[2] periodically inventory all stocks of controlled substances,[3] provide effective security controls,[4] and maintain records to account for all controlled substances manufactured, imported, exported, received, distributed, or otherwise disposed of.[5] DEA officials said that the closed system, including quotas, is designed to reduce the amount of pharmaceuticals that are diverted for illicit purposes, while also ensuring an adequate and uninterrupted supply of controlled substances for legitimate medical needs. They said that both legitimate and illegitimate users of prescription pain relievers often acquire the drugs from the same source—from doctors or other practitioners who prescribe or dispense them. For example, diversion of prescription pain relievers may occur through methods such as doctor shopping, thefts from medicine cabinets, improper prescribing, and forged prescriptions.

According to DEA, quotas are a tool used at the beginning of the closed system to manage and prevent diversion of controlled substances, such as the substances used to make prescription pain relievers, during their legitimate scientific, medical, and industrial applications. While DEA is authorized to control the overall amount of controlled substances available, according to DEA officials, it is ultimately for practitioners and their regulating bodies to ensure that these substances are prescribed appropriately. While officials said that they do seek to account for known diversion when setting APQs, they said that establishing quotas based on known diversion for the purpose of reducing the availability of prescribed drugs will not appreciably affect diversion at the retail level and may prevent legitimate patients from having access to medication for legitimate medical needs.

Aggregate Production Quotas

DEA officials said that the APQ is the first type of quota that DEA sets for each year.[6] The APQ specifies the maximum amount of each basic class of controlled substance listed in schedule I or II that can be produced for specified needs in the United States in a given year, thus limiting the amount of bulk raw materials available for use in the manufacture of prescription pain relievers. For example, methadone is a controlled substance that is used in the manufacture of drugs for addiction treatment as well as in the manufacture of the prescription pain relievers Dolophine and Methadose, and multiple generic equivalents. In 2010, DEA set the final APQ for methadone at 20,000,000 grams. Therefore, this is the maximum amount of methadone that could be available for manufacturing addiction treatment drugs and prescription pain relievers that use this substance, as well as for other authorized uses, in the United States in 2010.

DEA officials said that they consider data from many sources when determining the APQ, including estimates of the legitimate medical need for each substance from FDA, estimates of retail consumption based on prescriptions dispensed from IMS Health, companies' production history and forecasts, data from DEA's own internal system for tracking controlled substances transactions, and past quota histories for each substance.[7] DEA officials said that DEA scientists draw on their professional expertise and experience when considering all available data to recommend the appropriate APQ for a substance. DEA then publishes the proposed APQ for each substance for the following calendar year in the *Federal Register*, and, after receiving and reviewing comments, DEA publishes a final order determining the APQ for that year. DEA can revise the APQ midyear if legitimate changes in U.S. manufacturing requirements, such as increased sales or exports, new manufacturers entering the market, new product development, or product recalls, warrant a change. For example, in 2010, DEA revised the APQ for methadone, decreasing it from an initial APQ of 25,000,000 grams to the revised APQ of 20,000,000 grams.

Officials said that when determining the APQ they also consider losses of controlled substances that occur through diversion activities by considering known and reported thefts and losses, case seizures, and information from national databases of drug evidence, such as analysis from DEA and other forensic laboratories and law enforcement entities. DEA can reduce the APQ based on the quantity of seized or diverted material. The APQ may also be decreased because of DEA enforcement actions that impact sales data, such as by shutting down rogue pain clinics, thus reducing the amount of controlled substances purchased by such entities. DEA officials said that because sales data are one factor considered in determining APQ, these actions may ultimately lead to a reduction in the APQ. DEA said that in rare instances the APQ may also be increased as a result of diversion activities. For example, if a large quantity of a controlled substance is stolen from a manufacturer, the APQ may need to be raised to ensure that sufficient quantities of that substance will be available to meet the nation's ongoing legitimate medical needs. When determining the following year's APQ, DEA considers such circumstances to ensure that the APQ remains at an appropriate level to meet legitimate need and may reduce the APQ in relation to the previous year's to account for the known diversion.

Bulk Manufacturing Quotas and Procurement Quotas

In addition to the APQ, DEA sets two types of quotas for individual companies: bulk manufacturing quotas[8] and procurement quotas.[9] Bulk manufacturing quotas limit the amount of a basic class of schedule I or II controlled substance that an individual company can extract or synthesize from plant material or other controlled substances. According to DEA officials, once the initial APQ for a substance for a calendar year is set by DEA, individual companies apply to DEA for bulk manufacturing quotas for specific controlled substances to produce the bulk raw materials that are used in prescription pain relievers for that same year. Officials said that separate quotas are issued for each DEA-registered facility that manufactures a controlled substance, even if the same company operates multiple manufacturing facilities. In 2010, five facilities received bulk manufacturing quotas for methadone. The quota levels ranged between 4 grams at the low end and 12,000,000 grams at the highest levels. The sum of the bulk manufacturing quotas for all companies for a particular controlled substance cannot exceed the APQ for that substance in a given year.

DEA officials said that they use a variety of data sources—including internal DEA data, IMS Health data, and data provided by the company— to determine the bulk manufacturing quota for a company. DEA's Office of Diversion Control also reviews the company for any pending administrative, civil, or criminal action. DEA officials said that DEA scientists draw on their professional expertise and experience when considering all available data to recommend an appropriate bulk manufacturing quota, which is then issued to the company by letter. Bulk manufacturing quotas can be revised through a process similar to that used in setting the initial quotas, in that a company submits an application to revise its quota and must include supporting documentation. DEA officials said that DEA does not generally initiate changes to bulk manufacturing quotas on its own.

DEA also establishes procurement quotas, which limit the amount of a basic class of schedule I or II controlled substance that an individual company can procure from a manufacturer of bulk raw materials in order to manufacture individual dosage units of a medicine, such as a prescription pain reliever. Individual companies must apply to DEA for procurement quotas for each specific basic class of controlled substance, and DEA officials told us that separate quotas are issued for each facility that procures a controlled substance. For example, according to DEA data, 52 facilities received procurement quotas for methadone in 2010. The quota levels ranged between 1 gram at the low end and 9,000,000 grams at the highest levels. Sometimes an individual company may be engaged in both bulk manufacturing and procurement activities for the same controlled substance. In this case, the company will apply for both a bulk manufacturing quota and a procurement quota. DEA officials said they use the same process and data sources, as described above, to determine appropriate levels for procurement quotas as for bulk manufacturing quotas.

Officials said that DEA does not always set a company's bulk manufacturing quota or procurement quota at the level the company requested. For example, if a registrant is suspected of unlawfully diverting controlled substances, DEA will take this factor into consideration when determining whether to grant or deny the quota request. In addition, DEA may set the quota lower than requested if a company has set its quota request based on projected sales figures, which can inflate the quantity of quota requested, rather than on actual sales figures. DEA officials said that the agency uses actual sales and inventory figures in their evaluation of bulk manufacturing or procurement quota applications, and they grant quotas in line with legitimate medical need. In the past, we have reported that DEA cited difficulties in determining an appropriate level for quotas to ensure that adequate quantities are available for legitimate medical need, as there are not direct measures available to establish legitimate medical need. DEA officials said that, based on the available prescription and sales data, there is no method to calculate which prescriptions are issued for a legitimate medical purpose by a practitioner acting in the usual course of professional practice and which are not. They noted that if DEA were to reduce a quota level by some percentage to account for estimated illegitimate prescriptions or to otherwise reduce a quota by an amount estimating how much of the substance is abused and misused, the action would only reduce the total amount of substance available for dispensing, and would not affect to whom or in what quantities the drugs are prescribed or dispensed. Therefore, DEA officials said that a reduction in the supply of a drug based upon estimated illegitimate prescriptions or abuse and misuse could result in a shortage of the substance for legitimate purposes, while not affecting illicit demand for the substance at all. As a result, officials said that the agency does not use the quota process as a tool to reduce demand or to help prevent abuse and misuse of prescription pain relievers.

APPENDIX III: OBJECTIVES, SCOPE, AND METHODOLOGY

This report (1) describes recent national trends in prescription pain reliever abuse and misuse, (2) describes how federal agencies are educating prescribers about prescription pain reliever abuse and misuse, (3) assesses the extent to which federal agencies follow key practices for developing public education efforts about prescription pain reliever abuse and misuse, and (4) identifies educational efforts that use similar strategies and assess how agencies coordinate those efforts. To conduct this work we interviewed officials and reviewed documents, as described below for each objective. In addition, to gain context on the challenge of addressing the problem of abuse and misuse of prescription pain relievers while ensuring access to these pain relievers for legitimate medical use, we interviewed officials from the American Pain Foundation, and Purdue Pharma L.P., the manufacturer of the prescription pain reliever OxyContin.

To describe recent national trends in prescription pain reliever abuse and misuse, we interviewed officials from the Centers for Disease Control and Prevention (CDC), DEA, FDA, the National Institutes of Health's (NIH) National Institute on Drug Abuse (NIDA), the Office of National Drug Control Policy (ONDCP), and the Substance Abuse and Mental Health Services Administration (SAMHSA). We also conducted a literature review to identify relevant data sources and explanations for trends in prescription pain reliever abuse and misuse and analyzed data related to prescription pain reliever abuse and misuse from several data sources representative of the U.S. population aged 12 years and older. We included data in our review from the Drug Abuse Warning Network (DAWN), the National Vital Statistics System (NVSS), the Treatment Episode Data Set (TEDS), and the National Survey on Drug Use and Health (NSDUH). We selected these four data sources because they are the data sources that the agencies we interviewed use for monitoring trends in prescription pain reliever abuse and misuse, and because they are nationally representative.[1] We analyzed data for calendar years 2003- 2009, the most recent years for which data from at least three data sources were available.

DAWN, a public health surveillance system operated by SAMHSA, provides annual national estimates of drug-related emergency department visits, including visits involving the abuse or misuse of prescription pain relievers. [2] These national estimates are produced from data DAWN collects from a national sample of general, nonfederal hospitals operating 24-hour emergency departments. For each sample hospital, a trained DAWN reporter conducts a retrospective review of a random sample of emergency department medical records to identify emergency department visits that involved recent drug use. The number of visits may not directly represent the number of individuals who have visited emergency departments in a given year, since some patients may have more than one visit in a year. Emergency department medical records may vary in specificity and detail. For example, prescription pain reliever abuse and misuse may be overreported if the medical record is unclear about whether an individual was abusing or misusing a prescription pain reliever, or taking it as prescribed while abusing or misusing another drug. Conversely, prescription pain reliever abuse and misuse may be under-reported if the abuse or misuse of a regularly prescribed prescription pain reliever is not recognized or documented by the clinician. Because of changes to the DAWN methodology for 2004, we were not able to look at trends in DAWN data prior to that year.

NVSS, operated by CDC, receives and compiles data from all death certificates filed in the United States each year, including deaths involving prescription pain relievers. The causes of death section of the death certificates are completed by local medical examiners, coroners, or attending physicians, and the information is then coded by the states, or in some cases by CDC, and submitted to CDC, where it is further processed and coded, if necessary.[3] NVSS data on overdoses includes both the mechanism of injury leading to death (such as poisoning by certain substances) and the manner or intent, including unintentional, suicide, homicide, undetermined, and legal intervention or war. Although CDC sometimes reports on all manners of overdose deaths combined, we focused only on unintentional deaths because it matches most closely with our definition of abuse and misuse.[4] CDC officials said that some jurisdictions may undercount unintentional overdose deaths involving prescription pain relievers because of inconsistent use of toxicological lab tests, which may result in listing a death as a drug overdose death with no drugs specified on the death certificate, and other inconsistencies among jurisdictions, such as how they determine whether deaths are unintentional.[5] NVSS data for 2009 were not published in time for inclusion in this report.

TEDS, compiled by SAMHSA, gathers data on admissions to substance abuse treatment facilities nationwide, including data about the substances being abused by the person being admitted to treatment, such as prescription pain relievers. TEDS does not include all admissions to substance abuse treatment. It includes admissions at facilities that are licensed or certified by the state substance abuse agency to provide substance abuse treatment (or are administratively tracked for other reasons). In general, facilities reporting TEDS data are those that receive state alcohol or drug agency funds (including federal block grant funds) for the provision of alcohol or drug treatment services. Data about admissions are initially gathered by the facilities themselves and then collected by states and transmitted to a national data center. The number of admissions does not directly represent the number of individuals who have been admitted to treatment in a given year, because an individual admitted to treatment twice within a calendar year would be counted as two admissions. While treatment facilities included in TEDS account for a significant portion of treatment admissions nationwide, SAMHSA officials told us that no nationwide estimates are available of admissions to private, for-profit facilities or on the number of individuals being treated for substance abuse by physicians who have been approved to independently treat opioid addiction in an office-based setting. Therefore, SAMHSA officials told us that TEDS data underreport the number of individuals seeking treatment for prescription pain reliever abuse and misuse in the United States, especially among populations that have the resources to seek treatment from private facilities or physicians. In addition, the facilities and populations included in the data each state reports to TEDS are affected by state regulations and funding priorities. For example, some states report data from hospital- and prison-based treatment facilities, while others do not.

Finally, some states may target certain populations, such as teenagers, with their limited funds for addiction treatment, meaning that these populations may be more heavily represented in the data from those states.

NSDUH, an annual survey sponsored by SAMHSA, provides annual national estimates about the use of illicit drugs, alcohol, and tobacco in the civilian, noninstitutionalized population of the United States aged 12 years old or older, including estimates about the abuse and misuse of prescription pain relievers.[6] These national estimates are produced from data NSDUH collects through a national household survey, which involves in-person interviews with sampled respondents. SAMHSA officials reported that NSDUH may underestimate the extent of drug use, including prescription pain reliever abuse and misuse, both due to underreporting by surveyed individuals and because the sample may not include some individuals at high risk for drug use. We have reported on these limitations in the past.[7] While NSDUH incorporates strategies intended to increase respondents' cooperation and willingness to report honestly and accurately, such as use of computer-assisted interviewing methods, it is not possible to know the extent of underreporting within NSDUH data. However, SAMHSA officials told us that when looking at trended data, underreporting is not a problem because it is assumed constant.

To assess the reliability of these data for our purposes, we reviewed related documentation and conducted interviews with knowledgeable agency officials from CDC and SAMHSA to learn about data collection, quality control, and any limitations of these data sources. We also conducted electronic and manual data testing to ensure the quality of the data. We determined that all data we assessed were sufficiently reliable to provide overall trends for the purposes of our review.

To describe how federal agencies are educating prescribers about prescription pain reliever abuse and misuse, we reviewed the 2010 National Drug Control Strategy and interviewed officials involved with federal prevention efforts to identify strategies used to educate prescribers during fiscal year 2011. We then interviewed officials from FDA, NIH, and SAMHSA and reviewed agency websites and documents to describe educational strategies used by these agencies. Because they are involved in federal prevention efforts, we also interviewed officials from DEA, the Health Resources and Services Administration (HRSA), ONDCP, and the American Medical Association about gaps in current prescriber education efforts and efforts to fill these gaps through mandatory prescriber education. We excluded agencies that support their own health care systems, such as the Bureau of Prisons, Department of Defense, Indian Health Service, and Department of

Veterans Affairs, from the scope of our review as they serve special populations, rather than the general public. We also excluded educational efforts related to drug abuse treatment, including education about the use of the prescription pain relievers methadone or buprenorphine for use in the treatment of opioid addiction.

Table 3. Key Practices for Developing Public Education Efforts

Key practice	Description
Define goals and objectives	Define the goals of the communications campaign, e.g., to increase awareness or motivate a change in behavior. Define the objectives that will help the campaign meet those goals.
Analyze the situation	Analyze the situation, including any competing voices or messages, related market conditions, and key dates or timing constraints. Review relevant past experiences and examples to identify applicable "lessons learned" that may help to guide efforts.
Identify stakeholders	Identify and engage all the key stakeholders who will be involved in communications efforts. Clarify the roles and responsibilities of each stakeholder, including which entity or entities will lead overall efforts.
Identify resources	Identify available short- and long-term budgetary and other resources.
Research target audiences	Conduct audience research, such as dividing the audience into smaller groups of people who have relevant needs, preferences and characteristics, as well as measuring audience awareness, beliefs, competing behaviors, and motivators. Also, identify any potential audience-specific obstacles, such as access to information.
Develop consistent, clear messages	Determine what messages to develop based on budget, goals, and audience research findings. Develop clear and consistent audience messages; test and refine them.
Identify credible messenger(s)	Identify who will be delivering the messages and ensure that the source is credible with audiences.
Design media mix	Plan the media mix to optimize earned media (such as news stories or opinion editorials) and paid media (such as broadcast, print, or Internet advertising). Identify through which methods (e.g., advertising in newsprint ads), how often (e.g., weekly or monthly) and over what duration (e.g., 1 year) messages will reach audiences.
Establish metrics to measure success	Establish both process and outcome metrics to measure success in achieving objectives of the outreach campaign. Process metrics assure the quality, quantity, and timeliness of the contractor's work. Outcome metrics evaluate how well the campaign influenced the attitudesand behaviors of the target audience(s) that it set out to influence.

Source: GAO.

Note: See GAO, *Digital Television Transition: Increased Federal Planning and Risk Management Could Further Facilitate the DTV Transition*, GAO-08-43 (Washington, D.C.: Nov. 19, 2007).

To assess the extent to which federal agencies follow key practices for developing public education efforts about prescription pain reliever abuse and misuse, we reviewed the 2010 National Drug Control Strategy and interviewed officials involved with federal prevention efforts to identify efforts to educate the general public during fiscal year 2011. We then interviewed officials from DEA, FDA, NIH, ONDCP, and SAMHSA and reviewed agency websites and documents to gather evidence about how agencies developed public education efforts and then compared the development of these educational efforts against key practices for developing consumer education efforts from our prior work, *Digital Television Transition: Increased Federal Planning and Risk Management Could Further Facilitate the DTV Transition* (see table 3).[8] We also consulted the Department of Health and Human Services (HHS) publication, *Making Health Communications Programs Work*, for additional information about best practices for developing public education initiatives.[9] We also contacted the National Council on Patient Information and Education to gain information about best practices for public health education.

We limited our scope to efforts that target the general public, rather than specific populations, such as educational efforts pursued by the Department of Veterans Affairs, the Department of Defense, or the Indian Health Service. We also focused on efforts that were being actively revised or disseminated during fiscal year 2011. We focused on programs that craft targeted messages about abuse and misuse, rather than efforts that strictly provide factual information, such as drug fact websites and medication guides that come with prescription drugs, since our criteria for developing consumer education efforts are only appropriate for efforts that seek to convey a particular message.

To identify educational efforts that use similar strategies and assess how agencies coordinate those efforts, we interviewed officials from DEA, FDA, HRSA, NIH, ONDCP, and SAMHSA and reviewed documents about efforts to coordinate public and prescriber education initiatives. We then assessed these coordination activities against key practices for collaboration identified in our prior work.[10] We also assessed the extent to which agencies targeted similar populations, provided similar information, and used similar strategies to educate the general public and prescribers about prescription pain reliever abuse and misuse.

We conducted this performance audit from December 2010 through December 2011 in accordance with generally accepted government auditing standards. Those standards require that we plan and perform the audit to obtain sufficient, appropriate evidence to provide a reasonable basis for our findings and conclusions based on our audit objectives. We believe that the evidence obtained provides a reasonable basis for our findings and conclusions based on our audit objectives.

APPENDIX IV: PUBLIC EDUCATION PROGRAMS

We identified nine efforts in fiscal year 2011 to educate the general public about prescription pain reliever abuse and misuse (see table 4).

DEA	
Take Back Initiative	To promote DEA's drug collection program (National Take Back Day) and educate the public about drug disposal, DEA created web buttons, posters, brochures, billboards, and banners.
Get Smart About Drugs	A website for parents and caregivers to learn about drug abuse and to give them the tools to talk to their children about drugs. The website includes a downloadable booklet, *Prescription for Disaster: How Teens Abuse Medicine*, and educational PowerPoint presentations for community groups.
Just Think Twice	A website to educate teens about the dangers of drug abuse. It is intended to talk to teens in "their language" and give them the information they need to make informed decisions about drugs. The website also includes a teacher's guide that provides lesson plans and classroom activities about drug abuse.
Good Medicine, Bad Behavior	A museum exhibit that provides information on the history of prescription drug abuse anddiversion in the United States and efforts to combat the problem through time, including the effects of prescription drugs on the body and the dangers of misuse.
FDA	
Opioid Public Service Announcements	In-store broadcast announcements and a slide presentation shown in physician waiting rooms over a 4-week period. The announcements and slides contain messages about how to properly use, store, and dispose of prescription medications.
NIH	
Heads Up: Real News About Drugs and Your Body	Heads Up is a drug education series from Scholastic and NIH for teachers and 11- to 15-year-old students with materials about drugs' effects on the brain and body. The series includes inserts in Scholastic magazines and a presence on the Scholastic website and includes materials such as teacher guides and posters.
NIDA for Teens	Launched in 2003, NIDA for Teens provides teens with science-based information about the harmful effects that prescription drug abuse and addiction have on the brain and body through a website and hard copy materials. PEERx is the prescription drug abuse component within the NIDA for Teens website.
ONDCP	

Appendix IV. (Continued)

DEA	
National Youth Anti-Drug Media Campaign	Aims to prevent and reduce youth drug abuse across the nation through a mass-media campaign. The Campaign targets youth, their parents and other caregivers, and community organizations through two primary brands: *Above the Influence*is the Campaign's teen brand and *Parents. The Anti-Drug*is the Campaign's brand aimed at parents, other caregivers, and community organizations. In fiscal year 2011, the Campaign targeted parents and teens with messages about prescription drug abuse and misuse on its websites.
SAMHSA	
"Not Worth the Risk; Even if it's Legal"	A series of posters and brochures released in three phases targeting teens, college students, and teen influencers with information about the dangers of prescription drug abuse.

Source: GAO review of information from DEA, FDA, NIH, ONDCP, and SAMHSA.

Appendix V: Data from Key Measures of Prescription Pain Reliever Abuse and Misuse

To determine recent trends in prescription pain reliever abuse and misuse, we analyzed trends from 2003 to 2009 in four key measures used to monitor prescription pain reliever abuse and misuse. These measures include emergency department visits (see table 5), admissions to substance abuse treatment facilities (see table 6), and unintentional overdose deaths (see table 7) involving prescription pain relievers, as well as the number of individuals who reported abusing or misusing prescription pain relievers in the past year (see table 8).

Table 5. Estimated Number of Emergency Department Visits Related to Abuse and Misuse of Prescription Pain Relievers by Age Groups with Confidence Intervals, 2004-2009

		2004	2005	2006	2007	2008	2009[a]
12-15 years	Estimate	3,517	2,983	3,669	3,967	5,904	3,271
	Confidence Interval[b]	1,980 - 5,054	1,653 - 4,313	2,147 - 5,191	1,974 - 5,961	1,111- 10,696	1,391 - 5,151
16-19 years	Estimate	12,536	13,283	17,401	20,330	23,439	27,385
	Confidence Interval[b]	8,994 - 16,079	9,636 - 16,930	14,117 - 20,685	14,143 - 26,517	16,195 - 30,682	19,923 - 34,846

		2004	2005	2006	2007	2008	2009[a]
20-29 years	Estimate	43,912	60,074	70,763	81,318	117,744	134,682
	Confidence Interval [b]	31,501 - 56,322	45,911 - 74,237	56,519 - 85,007	62,892 - 99,744	65,024 - 170,463	79,592 - 189,771
30-39 years	Estimate	50,875	52,656	58,193	68,229	85,801	102,939
	Confidence Interval [b]	40,974 - 60,776	41,247 - 64,064	48,767 - 67,620	53,924 - 82,533	66,713 - 104,889	67,083 - 138,796
40-49 years	Estimate	51,542	63,789	71,742	81,724	95,991	98,454
	Confidence Interval [b]	39,342 - 63,742	50,548 - 77,029	63,385 - 80,099	66,827 - 96,621	74,972 - 117,010	78,221 - 118,686
50-59 years	Estimate	24,827	37,867	39,993	50,778	59,287	77,368
	Confidence Interval [b]	18,353 - 31,301	28,792 - 46,942	33,819 - 46,166	41,885 - 59,670	47,981 - 70,593	63,016 - 91,720
60+ years	Estimate	14,950	18,505	22,310	27,403	39,928	45,852
	Confidence Interval [b]	9,777 - 20,123	12,911 - 24,099	16,812 - 27,809	21,284 - 33,521	30,285 - 49,571	36,776 - 54,929
Total (12+ years)	**Estimate**	**202,159**	**249,156**	**284,071**	**333,748**	**428,092**	**489,951**
	Confidence Interval [b]	**159,527 -244,791**	**199,241 -299,070**	**246,132 -322,011**	**277,696 -389,800**	**314,570 - 541,614**	**358,177 - 621,724**

Source: Drug Abuse Warning Network (DAWN), Substance Abuse and Mental Health Services Administration (SAMHSA).

Notes: SAMHSA defines emergency department visits related to abuse and misuse of prescription pain relievers broadly to include all visits involving nonmedical use of a prescription pain reliever (such as when a patient exceeded prescribed or recommended dose, used drugs prescribed for another individual, or was administered a drug by another person for a malicious purpose) or use of a prescription pain reliever in combination with alcohol or illicit drugs.

DAWN data represent visits, not unique individuals; thus, an individual who visits an emergency department twice within a calendar year would be counted as two visits. Comparable emergency department visit estimates are not available for 2003 because changes were made that year to the data collection methodology.

[a] The change from 2004 to 2009 is statistically significant at the 95 percent confidence level for all age groups except for the 12-15 years age group.

[b] This table presents the lower and upper bounds of a 95 percent confidence level for each estimate.

Table 6. Number of Admissions to Substance Abuse Treatment Facilities for Prescription Pain Reliever Abuse and Misuse by Age Groups, 2003-2009

	2003	**2004**	**2005**	**2006**	**2007**	**2008**	**2009**
12-15 years	1,308	1,406	1,513	1,489	1,847	2,440	2,786
16-19 years	6,653	8,041	8,825	9,717	11,367	15,213	18,322
20-29 years	32,132	39,518	48,882	59,880	71,522	89,485	104,650
30-39 years	28,612	30,250	33,604	37,232	42,251	50,525	56,474
40-49 years	24,575	25,827	27,512	29,402	30,630	33,378	34,059
50-59 years	6,998	7,975	9,500	10,952	12,752	15,170	15,820
60+ years	915	1,047	1,213	1,333	1,556	1,911	2,133
Total (12+ years)	**101,193**	**114,064**	**131,049**	**150,005**	**171,925**	**208,122**	**234,244**

Source: Treatment Episode Data Set (TEDS), Substance Abuse and Mental Health Services Administration.

Note: Admissions for prescription pain reliever abuse and misuse include all admissions where methadone (not prescribed for the individual) or other non-heroin opioids were reported as primary, secondary, or tertiary substances of abuse at the time of admission. TEDS data represents admissions, not unique individuals; thus, an individual admitted to treatment twice within a calendar year would be counted as two admissions.

Table 7. Number of Unintentional Overdose Deaths Involving Prescription Pain Relievers by Age Groups, 2003-2008

	2003	**2004**	**2005**	**2006**	**2007**	**2008**
12-15 years	a	37	29	32	51	36
16-19 years	207	269	248	350	361	366
20-29 years	1,053	1,341	1,547	2,154	2,314	2,291
30-39 years	1,566	1,633	1,874	2,394	2,464	2,469
40-49 years	2,448	2,777	2,983	3,581	3,519	3,541
50-59 years	1,001	1,217	1,510	2,083	2,338	2,612
60+ years	218	267	343	392	462	562
Total (12+ years)	**6,493**[b]	**7,541**	**8,534**	**10,986**	**11,509**	**11,877**

Source: GAO analysis of National Vital Statistics System multiple cause of death mortality files, Centers for Disease Control and Prevention.

Notes: Deaths resulting from unintentional overdoses of prescription pain relievers are defined as those with an underlying cause of death of poisoning (International Classification of Diseases, Tenth Revision (ICD-10) code of X40-X49) and any mention of ICD-10 codes T40.2, T40.3, or T40.4 as a multiple cause. These data do not include deaths in which drugs are present but the cause of death was determined to be something other than poisoning, such as cancer or motor vehicle traffic crashes. Data represents U.S. residents only. Unintentional overdose deaths data from 2009 were not published in time for this report.

[a] Fewer than 20 deaths. Does not meet standards of reliability or precision.

[b] The total for 2003 does not include deaths of individuals aged 12-15 years, because there were fewer than 20 deaths in this age group.

Table 8. Estimated Number of Individuals Who Reported Abusing or Misusing Prescription Pain Relievers in the Past Year by Age Groups with Confidence Intervals, 2003-2009 (in Thousands)

		2003	2004	2005	2006	2007	2008	2009
12-15 years[a]	Estimate	927	933	797	879	786	750	772
	Confidence Interval[b]	851 - 1,008	855 - 1,017	725 - 875	803 - 963	712 - 868	679 - 829	701 - 850
16-19 years	Estimate	2,152	2,136	2,169	2,151	2,095	1,981	2,005
	Confidence Interval[b]	2,025 - 2,285	2,009 - 2,269	2,044 - 2,300	2,025 - 2,283	1,964 - 2,233	1,853 - 2,116	1,887 - 2,130
20-29 years[a]	Estimate	3,797	3,804	3,943	4,341	4,049	4,136	4,306
	Confidence Interval[b]	3,560 - 4,048	3,563 - 4,060	3,690 - 4,212	4,062 - 4,637	3,802 - 4,309	3,874 - 4,413	4,031 - 4,597
30-39 years	Estimate	2,128	1,923	2,107	2,151	2,293	1,962	2,135
	Confidence Interval[b]	1,869 - 2,421	1,686 - 2,192	1,843 - 2,405	1,897 - 2,437	2,007 - 2,617	1,710 - 2,249	1,870 - 2,436
40-49 years	Estimate	1,815	1,703	1,566	1,974	1,767	1,792	1,645
	Confidence Interval[b]	1,541 – 2,135	1,468 - 1,973	1,329 - 1,843	1,701 - 2,288	1,536 - 2,031	1,552 - 2,067	1,410 - 1,917
50-59 years[a]	Estimate	514	590	876	882	1,070	759	1,193
	Confidence Interval[b]	350 - 754	419 - 830	641 - 1,195	671 - 1,157	796 - 1,435	558 - 1,030	921 - 1,543
60+ years	Estimate	338	167	358	272	406	506	349
	Confidence Interval[b]	192 - 593	97 – 289	221 - 580	159 - 462	258 - 639	337 - 757	225 - 539
Total (12+ years)	**Estimate**	**11,671**	**11,256**	**11,815**	**12,649**	**12,466**	**11,885**	**12,405**
	Confidence Interval[b]	**11,096 - 12,273**	**10,695 - 11,844**	**11,233 - 12,426**	**12,063 - 13,263**	**11,861 - 13,100**	**11,319 - 12,479**	**11,788 - 13,052**

Source: National Survey on Drug Use and Health, Substance Abuse and Mental Health Services Administration.

Notes: These estimates are based on the number of survey respondents who reported using a prescription pain reliever not prescribed for the respondent or used only for the experience or feeling it caused in the past 12 months prior to the survey being conducted.

The survey results are weighted to represent the U.S. civilian, noninstitutionalized population.

[a] The change from 2003 to 2009 is statistically significant at the 95 percent confidence level for only the 12-15 years, 20-29 years, and 50-59 years age groups.

[b] This table presents the lower and upper bounds of a 95 percent confidence level for each estimate.

End Notes

[1] According to NSDUH data from 2009, 17 percent of these people reported that they got the drug from one doctor and 2 percent reported that they got the drug from more than one doctor.

[2] In this report the term "prescription pain relievers" refers to a class of pain relievers known as opioid analgesics. While multiple classes of pain relievers are used in the United States, opioid analgesics, such as fentanyl, hydrocodone, methadone, morphine, and oxycodone, are the most commonly abused and misused pain relievers. In addition to relieving pain, they can cause feelings of euphoria or a sense of well being among some people who take them, which may lead to their abuse and misuse.

[3] No standard definitions of prescription pain reliever abuse or prescription pain reliever misuse are used by the federal agencies dealing with these issues. In this report, we use the term "abuse and misuse" to collectively refer to the three types of inappropriate use most often included in the agencies' definitions: using a prescription pain reliever with the intent to get high, with or without a prescription of one's own; using a prescription pain reliever for pain relief, but without a prescription of one's own; or using a prescription pain reliever for pain relief, with a prescription of one's own, but in ways other than as prescribed, such as by taking more than prescribed.

[4] GAO, *Methadone-Associated Overdose Deaths: Factors Contributing to Increased Deaths and Efforts to Prevent Them*, GAO-09-341 (Washington, D.C.: Mar. 26, 2009) and *Prescription Drugs: OxyContin Abuse and Diversion and Efforts to Address the Problem*, GAO-04-110 (Washington, D.C.: Dec. 23, 2003). For more GAO reports on this topic, see the Related GAO Products page at the end of this report.

[5] GAO, *Digital Television Transition: Increased Federal Planning and Risk Management Could Further Facilitate the DTV Transition*, GAO-08-43 (Washington, D.C.: Nov. 19, 2007).

[6] GAO, *Results-Oriented Government: Practices that Can Help Enhance and Sustain Collaboration among Federal Agencies,* GAO-06-15 (Washington, D.C.: Oct. 21, 2005).

[7] Other activities at the federal level are beyond the scope of our review, including prevention activities like supporting state prescription drug monitoring programs— programs that collect information on prescription drugs that are prescribed or dispensed in a state in order to detect and prevent the abuse and misuse of these drugs—and enabling safe disposal of prescription drugs; federal efforts to expand access to addiction treatment; and federal law enforcement activities, such as taking action against "pill mills" where prescription pain relievers can be obtained without a legitimate medical need.

[8] A report from the Institute of Medicine stated that more than 100 million Americans are affected by chronic pain. Institute of Medicine, *Relieving Pain In America: A Blueprint for Transforming Prevention, Care, Education, and Research* (Washington, D.C.: The National Academies Press, 2011).

[9] There are also particular prescription pain relievers, such as methadone, that are referred to as long-acting, rather than extended-release, because they deliver drugs to the body for a longer period of time due to inherent characteristics of the drug substance, rather than because of being specially formulated for an extended period of drug release.

[10] Some individuals may also abuse or misuse prescription pain relievers by using pain relievers that were not prescribed to them in order to prevent drug withdrawal symptoms, which may occur if an individual stops or dramatically reduces use of prescription pain relievers after heavy and prolonged use.

[11] DEA officials told us that in addition to federal laws and regulations, state laws and medical practice standards govern the prescribing of prescription drugs. These state laws and standards may include requiring tamper-resistant prescribing pads and restricting who can prescribe controlled substances.

[12] Pub. L. No. 91-513, 84 Stat. 1242 (1970) (codified at 21 U.S.C. §§ 801 et seq. as amended). Under the Controlled Substances Act drugs are placed into one of five schedules based on their accepted medicinal uses and potential for abuse and dependence. Schedule I and II drugs have the highest potential for abuse and dependence, and schedules III through V have progressively lower potential for abuse and dependence.

See 21 U.S.C. §812. All drugs in schedules II through V are available to the public with a prescription. *See* 21 U.S.C. §829. In addition, some schedule V drugs may be available to the public without a prescription, but subject to certain other restrictions.

[13] L. Mezei and B.B. Murinson, "Pain Education in North American Medical Schools," *Journal of Pain* (2011).

[14] According to the American Medical Association publication *State Medical Licensure Requirements and Statistics, 2012* the states in which medical boards required CME related to education on controlled substance prescribing or pain management for certain prescribers were California, Florida, Massachusetts (for license renewals after January 1, 2012), Oklahoma, Oregon, Rhode Island, Tennessee, Texas, and West Virginia.

[15] GAO-08-43. These key practices include: define key goals and objectives; analyze the situation; identify stakeholders; identify resources; research target audiences; develop clear, consistent messages; identify credible messenger(s); design a mix of media; and establish metrics to measure success. For further description of these key practices, see app. III.

[16] Diversion is the channeling of pharmaceuticals for illegal purposes or abuse. Diversion can involve illegal sales of prescription drugs by physicians, patients, or pharmacists, as well as obtaining controlled substances from Internet pharmacies without a valid prescription. Diversion can also involve such activities as "doctor shopping" by individuals who visit numerous physicians to obtain multiple prescriptions, prescription forgery, and pharmacy theft. For more on federal efforts to address the diversion of prescription drugs for illegal purposes or abuse, see GAO, *Medicare Part D: Instances of Questionable Access to Prescription Drugs*, GAO-11-699 (Washington, D.C.: Sept. 6, 2011); and *Prescription Drug Control: DEA Has Enhanced Efforts to Combat Diversion, but Could Better Assess and Report Program Results*, GAO-11-744 (Washington, D.C.: Aug. 26, 2011).

[17] DEA, NIH, ONDCP, and SAMHSA officials told us that they also use data from Monitoring the Future, an annual national survey supported by a grant from NIH's NIDA and administered to nationally representative samples of public and private secondary school students throughout the United States. (Monitoring the Future also includes surveys following high school students into adulthood.) We did not include this data source in our analysis because it primarily focuses on youth and young adults, and is thus not nationally representative at all age levels.

[18] NSDUH defines "nonmedical use" of a prescription drug as use without a prescription of the individual's own or simply for the experience or feeling the drugs caused. Such use would be included in our use of the term "abuse and misuse," though it only represents two of the three scenarios within that definition. It does not represent individuals who incorrectly use prescription pain relievers for pain relief, with a prescription of one's own, but in ways other than as prescribed, such as by taking more than prescribed.

[19] See app. V for the estimated number of emergency department visits, admissions to substance abuse treatment facilities, and unintentional overdose deaths for each year analyzed along with the corresponding confidence intervals, where applicable.

[20] In 2004, according to DAWN, there were an estimated 202,000 emergency department visits related to prescription pain reliever abuse and misuse and an estimated 490,000 such visits in 2009. Comparable emergency department visit estimates are not available for 2003 because changes were made that year to the data collection methodology.

[21] In 2003, according to TEDS, there were about 101,000 admissions to substance abuse treatment facilities for prescription pain reliever abuse and misuse and about 234,000 such visits in 2009.

[22] In 2003 there were approximately 6,500 deaths resulting from unintentional overdoses of prescription pain relievers and approximately 11,900 such deaths in 2008. NVSS unintentional overdose deaths data from 2009 were not published in time for this report. The determination of intentionality in an overdose death is made by the attending physician, medical examiner, or coroner responsible for completing the causes of death section of the death certificate.

[23] National estimates of the number of people who abused and misused prescription pain relievers represent only two of the three scenarios that we defined as abuse and misuse. Estimates do not represent individuals who incorrectly use prescription pain relievers for pain relief, with a prescription of one's own, but in ways other than as prescribed, such as by taking more than prescribed. In addition, estimates do not differentiate between individuals who abused or misused a pain reliever with the intent to get high and those who abused or misused a pain reliever to relieve pain.

[24] The increase from 2003 to 2009 in the estimated number of people in the U.S. population aged 12 and older who abused and misused prescription pain relievers as reported in NSDUH is not statistically significant at the 95 percent confidence level. See app. V for the estimates for each year analyzed along with the corresponding confidence intervals.

[25] The estimates represent the number of prescriptions dispensed from U.S. outpatient retail pharmacies for non-injectable opioid analgesics, rounded to the nearest million. These estimates were obtained from FDA, based on its analysis of data from the SDI, Vector One®:National database, which measures retail dispensing of prescriptions based on a sample of retail pharmacies throughout the United States. The data were extracted from the database in June 2010.

[26] According to NSDUH, among persons aged 12 or older in 2009 who abused or misused a pain reliever in the past year, 19 percent got the drug that was most recently abused or misused as a prescription from a doctor. In addition, 55 percent got the drug they most recently abused or misused from a friend or relative for free, 11 percent bought the drug from a friend or relative, and 4 percent took the drug from a friend or relative without asking.

[27] From 2003 to 2009, prescriptions for extended-release and long-acting pain relievers increased from approximately 15 million to 23 million. Estimates of dispensed prescriptions are from FDA's analysis of SDI, Vector One®:National, extracted June 2010.

[28] FDA estimated that in 2008, there were 106.8 emergency department visits involving abuse or misuse of extended-release oxycodone for every 10,000 retail prescriptions, in contrast to 14.3 emergency department visits involving abuse or misuse of immediate-release oxycodone for every 10,000 retail prescriptions.

FDA developed these estimates based on an analysis of data from DAWN and SDI, Vector One®: National, extracted June 2010.

[29] Methadone has unique pharmacological properties that make it different from other opioids, and as a result, when it is used without adequate knowledge or when it is used for a purpose other than that for which it was prescribed, it can lead to adverse health consequences, including death. GAO-09-341.

[30] L.R. Webster et al., "An Analysis of the Root Causes for Opioid-Related Overdose Deaths in the United States," *Pain Medicine,* vol. 12 (2011).

[31] According to DAWN, in 2004, there were an estimated 63,000 emergency department visits involving a prescription pain reliever alone and an estimated 140,000 visits with both a prescription pain reliever and alcohol or other drugs. In 2009 these figures were estimated at 151,000 and 340,000, respectively.

[32] According to FDA, the course will be provided by organizations accredited to provide CME to physicians or by organizations that provide CE to health care professionals other than physicians.

[33] *See* Food and Drug Administration Amendments Act of 2007, Pub. L. No., 110-85, § 901, 121 Stat. 823, 922 (codified in pertinent part at 21 U.S.C. §§ 355(p), 355-1) (conditioning authority to market a drug on compliance with an approved REMS, where determined necessary to ensure the benefits outweigh the risks).

A REMS is a risk management plan that FDA can require a manufacturer to develop to manage serious risks associated with a drug. Prescription pain relievers subject to the extended-release and long-acting class-wide REMS include extended-release products containing buprenorphine, fentanyl, hydromorphone, morphine, oxycodone, oxymorphone, and tapentadol, and products containing the long-acting prescription pain reliever methadone.

[34] As the five products are highly potent and designed for transmucosal absorption they are only indicated for use in adults with breakthrough cancer pain who are already routinely taking another prescription pain reliever around the clock.

However, FDA officials told us that in studying the postmarket data, they became concerned that these drugs were being used in patients who were not already routinely taking another prescription pain reliever. Because these products have a very high risk of death if administered incorrectly or if taken by patients who were not already routinely taking another prescription pain reliever, FDA has also placed special restrictions on the dispensing of these products through REMS.

[35] Patient-prescriber agreements are documents signed by the patient and prescriber that outline patient and prescriber responsibilities, including, in the case of transmucosal immediate-release fentanyl products, documenting that the patient is regularly taking another prescription pain reliever and has been counseled on the risks, benefits, and appropriate use of these drugs.

[36] SAMHSA also funds two additional physician clinical support systems related to the use of methadone and buprenorphine in addiction treatment, which are outside the scope of our review.

[37] SAMHSA also provided funding to one additional medical residency program, but officials told us that the curriculum resources that residency program is developing do not include information about prescription drug abuse and misuse.

[38] *See* 21 U.S.C. § 823(f).

[39] GAO-08-43.

[40] In September 2010 DEA conducted a National Prescription Drug Take Back Day to provide a venue for the disposal of unwanted and unused prescription drugs. DEA held a second Take Back Day in April 2011 and a third in October 2011. A DEA official told us that such

events are a short-term measure until the agency can implement regulations for the Secure and Responsible Drug Disposal Act of 2010, which will allow for authorized entities to collect and dispose of controlled substances.

[41] The *National Youth Anti-Drug Media Campaign* (the Campaign) is a mass-media campaign, including paid advertising and public communications outreach. In fiscal year 2011, the Campaign targeted parents and teens with messages about prescription drug abuse and misuse on its websites, rather than through paid advertising.
The budget for the Campaign includes funding for all aspects of the Campaign. Only a small portion of the overall budget was spent on programming about prescription drug abuse.

[42] U.S. Department of Health and Human Services, National Institutes of Health and National Cancer Institute, *Making Health Communication Programs Work: A Planner's Guide* (2004).

[43] The tracking studies also evaluate teen awareness and memory of the Campaign's advertisements. However, there were no advertisements about prescription drug abuse and misuse being broadcast during fiscal year 2011.

[44] ONDCP awarded the evaluation contract to Westat, Inc. in July, 2010. We have previously reported on a prior Westat evaluation of the *National Youth Anti-Drug Media Campaign*; see GAO, *ONDCP Media Campaign: Contractor's National Evaluation Did Not Find that the Youth Anti-Drug Media Campaign Was Effective in Reducing Youth Drug Use*, GAO-06-818 (Washington, D.C.: Aug. 25, 2006).

[45] GAO, *Program Evaluation: Strategies for Assessing How Information Dissemination Contributes to Agency Goals*, GAO-02-923 (Washington, D.C.: Sept. 30, 2002).

[46] A Call to Action is a science-based document to stimulate action nationwide to solve a major public health problem.

[47] We have previously defined "duplication" as occurring when two or more agencies or programs are engaged in the same activities or provide the same services to the same beneficiaries.
GAO, *Opportunities to Reduce Potential Duplication in Government Programs, Save Tax Dollars, and Enhance Revenue,* GAO-11-318SP (Washington, D.C.: Mar. 1, 2011).

[48] These key practices are (1) defining and articulating a common outcome; (2) establishing mutually reinforcing or joint strategies; (3) identifying and addressing needs by leveraging resources; (4) agreeing on roles and responsibilities; (5) establishing compatible policies, procedures, and other means to operate across agency boundaries; (6) developing mechanisms to monitor, evaluate, and report on results; (7) reinforcing agency accountability for collaborative efforts through agency plans and reports; and (8) reinforcing individual accountability for collaborative efforts through performance management systems.
See GAO-06-15.

[49] The five goals are (1) improve the federal surveillance capacity for pharmaceutical abuse; (2) improve clinical outcomes for substance abusers by increasing access to prescription drug monitoring program data by clinicians in a timely manner and across state boundaries; (3) reduce the number of opioid overdose deaths by identifying and implementing effective secondary prevention strategies; (4) collaborate on the development of educational materials for health care providers, patients, parents, and communities at large to address the appropriate use of prescription pharmaceuticals and reduce their misuse and abuse; and (5) implement standards for electronic medical records to increase the identification of pharmaceutical abuse routinely in medical care.

End Notes for Appendix I

[1] Throughout this report we use the term "abuse and misuse" to collectively refer to the three types of inappropriate use that are most frequently incorporated into agencies definitions. However, in this appendix, because the literature we reviewed used the term "abuse," we use that term alone.

[2] To develop the list of types of abuse-deterrent formulations, we conducted a literature review. The following articles were particularly useful in defining the five types of abuse-deterrent formulations, and challenges associated with them, referenced here: J.J. Coleman, C.R. Schuster, and R.L. DuPont, "Reducing the Abuse Potential of Controlled Substances," *Pharmaceutical Medicine*, vol. 24, no. 1 (2010); J.J. Coleman, P.B. Bensiger, M.S. Gold, D.E. Smith, R.P. Bianchi, and R.L. DuPont, "Can Drug Design Inhibit Abuse?" *Journal of Psychoactive Drugs*, vol. 37, no. 4 (2005); N. Katz, "Abuse-deterrent Opioid Formulations: Are They a Pipe Dream?" *Current Rheumatology Reports,* vol. 10 (2008); J.P. Schneider, M. Matthews, and R.N. Jamison, "Abuse-Deterrent and Tamper-Resistant Opioid Formulations: What is their Role in Addressing Prescription Opioid Abuse?" *CNS Drugs*, vol. 24, no. 10 (2010); L. Webster, "Update on Abuse-Resistant and Abuse-Deterrent Approaches to Opioid Formulations," *Pain Medicine*, vol. 10, supplement 2 (2009); and N. P. Katz et. al., "Challenges in the Development of Prescription Opioid Abuse-deterrent Formulations," *Clinical Journal of Pain*, vol. 23, no. 8 (2007).

[3] One additional product, Suboxone, uses an agonist/antagonist combination to deter abuse, but this drug is indicated for the treatment of opioid dependence, not the treatment of pain. In addition, though it was marketed earlier in the year, in March 2011 Embeda was voluntarily recalled because a prespecified stability requirement was not met during routine testing. As of October 2011 the recall was still in effect, but Pfizer officials said they hope to return the product to market once the stability issue has been resolved.

[4] Though no prescription pain relievers that use aversion alone are currently marketed, in June 2011 FDA approved the prescription pain reliever Oxecta, which Pfizer officials said is designed to use a combination of physical/chemical barriers and aversion to deter abuse.

End Notes for Appendix II

[1] Controlled substances used in the manufacture of prescription pain relievers include codeine, fentanyl, hydrocodone, hydromorphone, methadone, morphine, oxycodone, and oxymorphone.

[2] 21 C.F.R. § 1301.11(a) (2011) (researchers are defined as manufacturers for purposes of this provision) (exemptions, such as institutions operated by the U.S. military, provided for at 21 C.F.R. §§ 1301.22 et seq. (2011)).

[3] *See* 21 C.F.R. §§ 1304.3, 1304.11 (2011).

[4] *See* 21 C.F.R. § 1301.71 (2011).

[5] *See* 21 C.F.R. § 1304.22 (2011).

[6] *See* 21 C.F.R. § 1303.11(a) (2011).

[7] DEA obtains data from the IMS Health National Prescription Audit. IMS Health is a private company that provides market information to the pharmaceutical and health care industries.

[8] *See* 21 C.F.R. § 1303.21 (2011). Although this regulation uses the term "individual manufacturing quotas," DEA officials refer to them as "bulk manufacturing quotas." Accordingly, we use the term "bulk manufacturing quotas" throughout our discussion.

[9] *See* 21 C.F.R. § 1303.12 (2011).

End Notes for Appendix III

[1] Although all of these data sources are nationally representative, they represent slightly different populations. For example, active military personnel are included to different extents in each of the data sources. NSDUH excludes active military personnel from its sample population. NVSS includes deaths of active military personnel, though it does not include overseas military deaths. DAWN and TEDS do not explicitly exclude active military personnel, though emergency department visits and treatment admissions at military-funded facilities are not included in these data sets. A DAWN official said that he therefore expects the number of individuals in the military included in these data to be low because these individuals likely use military-funded services. SAMHSA reports also note that the excluded populations may have different rates of prescription pain reliever abuse and misuse than the general public as a whole.

[2] Data on emergency department visits related to abuse and misuse may include cases of malicious poisoning, which is not included in our definition of abuse and misuse. However, SAMHSA officials told us that there are very few cases of malicious poisoning each year.

[3] NVSS data are coded in accordance with the International Classification of Diseases, Tenth Revision.

[4] Data on unintentional overdose deaths may include deaths that are not related to abuse and misuse, such as cases of unintentional ingestion of a prescription pain reliever. However, a CDC official said that these cases likely comprise only a small portion of unintentional overdose deaths.

[5] According to CDC analyses, in 2006, more than 20 percent of all drug overdose deaths did not specify the drugs involved.

[6] Specifically, NSDUH gathers information on the nonmedical use of prescription pain relievers, which it defines as the use of prescription pain relievers without a prescription of the individual's own or simply for the experience or feeling the drugs caused.

[7] GAO, *Drug Use Measurement: Strengths, Limitations, and Recommendations for Improvement,* GAO/PEMD-93-18 (Washington, D.C.: June 25, 1993).

[8] GAO-08-43.

[9] U.S. Department of Health and Human Services, National Institutes of Health and National Cancer Institute, *Making Health Communication Programs Work: A Planner's Guide* (2004).

[10] In our prior work, we identified key practices that help enhance and sustain collaboration. These key practices are (1) defining and articulating a common outcome; (2) establishing mutually reinforcing or joint strategies; (3) identifying and addressing needs by leveraging resources; (4) agreeing on roles and responsibilities; (5) establishing compatible policies, procedures, and other means to operate across agency boundaries; (6) developing mechanisms to monitor, evaluate, and report on results; (7) reinforcing agency accountability for collaborative efforts through agency plans and reports; and (8) reinforcing individual accountability for collaborative efforts through performance management systems. See GAO-06-15.

In: Prescription Drugs
Editors: J. J. Phillips and W. O. Penny
ISBN 978-1-62081-211-2

Chapter 2

PRESCRIPTION DRUG CONTROL: DEA HAS ENHANCED EFFORTS TO COMBAT DIVERSION, BUT COULD BETTER ASSESS AND REPORT PROGRAM RESULTS*

United States Government Accountability Office

WHY GAO DID THIS STUDY

The Drug Enforcement Administration's (DEA) Diversion Control Program is responsible for enforcing the Controlled Substances Act (CSA) and ensuring the availability of prescription drugs such as pain relievers and stimulants while preventing their diversion for abuse. The CSA requires entities handling controlled substances—such as manufacturers, pharmacies, and physicians, among others-- to register with DEA, which conducts regulatory investigations of registrants, as well as criminal investigations. GAO was asked (1) how DEA manages diversion investigation efforts, and (2) how DEA ensures policies and procedures are followed for investigations and the extent to which it determines the results of its efforts. GAO reviewed DEA policies and procedures, and interviewed DEA, state, and local officials at eleven

* This is an edited, reformatted and augmented version of a United States Government Accountability Office Publication No. GAO-11-744, dated August 2011.

locations which were selected on the basis of volume of cases handled, geographic diversity, and other considerations. These observations are not generalizable, but provided insights on DEA operations.

WHAT GAO RECOMMENDS

GAO recommends DEA reassess the program's performance measures to better link them to the goal of reducing diversion. DEA did not concur. GAO continues to believe the measures could be enhanced as discussed in this report.

WHAT GAO FOUND

To respond to the increasing rate of criminal diversion of prescription drugs and a growing registrant population, DEA has expanded its resources and targeted its investigation strategies to collaborate with state and local entities and enhance the effectiveness of its diversion investigations. Specifically, the agency expanded its use of Tactical Diversion Squads (squads) of DEA personnel as well as other federal, state, and local partners investigating diversion schemes to maximize resources and improve efforts to investigate criminal diversion. DEA currently has 40 squads across the country and plans to establish more. According to squad participants and DEA officials GAO contacted, the squads have improved communication and coordination and simplified information sharing for investigations. Because of the growing registrant population and noncompliance by some with the CSA and implementing regulations, DEA renewed its focus on regulatory oversight of registrants to better ensure compliance. By using the squads to free up resources previously dedicated to both criminal and regulatory cases, DEA used those resources to increase regulatory investigations of the registrants. As a result, the number of regulatory investigations more than tripled between fiscal years 2009 and 2010. DEA also conducted outreach to specific registrant types to inform them of regulatory responsibilities and prepare them for regulatory investigations.

DEA has taken steps to ensure that investigators follow policies and procedures for such investigations, but could better assess how its efforts are reducing the diversion of prescription drugs. To ensure that diversion investigators and special agents have the necessary skills to carry out their responsibilities and that DEA monitors the extent to which policies and procedures are followed during investigations, DEA has established internal controls related to guidance, training, and oversight of investigations. These controls include providing and updating guidance to investigators to follow during investigations, providing initial and on-going training to investigators, and monitoring the quality of investigations through a combination of direct supervisory reviews, self-inspections, and on-site internal inspections by DEA's Office of Inspections. Recent reports from on-site internal inspections of each of DEA's field divisions did not identify any widespread or systematic issues related to the timeliness and overall quality of diversion investigations. Given DEA's increased focus on investigations in response to growing prescription drug diversion, it is critical for DEA to determine the extent to which these additional efforts are reducing diversion. DEA has established performance measures for the Diversion Control Program, but these measures do not clearly demonstrate the effect the additional efforts are having on the diversion problem the program seeks to address. For example, for its overall performance measure of the diversion control program, DEA is tracking the development and implementation of an internal information technology project. By more closely linking performance measures to the goal of reducing diversion, DEA could better capture the results of the Diversion Control program to help inform decision makers in allocating resources.

Abbreviations

ARCOS	Automated Reports and Consolidated Orders System
CSA	Controlled Substances Act
CPOT	Consolidated Priority Organization Target
DEA	Drug Enforcement Administration
DOJ	Department of Justice
DWP	Drug Addiction Treatment Act waived physician
FBI	Federal Bureau of Investigation
HHS	Department of Health and Human Services
IRS	Internal Revenue Service
OMB	Office of Management and Budget
ONDCP	Office of National Drug Control Policy
PTO	Priority Target Organization
RapTOR	Rapid Targeting Online Reports Tool
SIP	Self-Inspection Program

August 26, 2011

The Honorable Chaka Fattah
Ranking Member
Subcommittee on Commerce,
Justice, Science and Related Agencies
Committee on Appropriations
House of Representatives

The Honorable C.A. Dutch Ruppersberger
House of Representatives

According to the Office of National Drug Control Policy (ONDCP), the abuse of controlled prescription drugs such as pain relievers, depressants, and stimulants is the nation's fastest-growing drug problem. Although such prescription drugs have legitimate medical uses, they also pose a potential for abuse and addiction and, thus, being diverted for nonmedical illicit uses. To prevent diversion, the Controlled Substances Act (CSA) was enacted in 1970 to regulate and facilitate the use of controlled substances, including certain drugs, for legitimate medical, scientific, research, and industrial purposes while preventing them from being diverted for illegal uses.[1] However, according to recent government data, the diversion of such drugs has risen in recent years as have the corresponding prevalence of addiction and the cost of lives lost. ONDCP has reported that prescription drugs now rank second for the most commonly abused category of drugs, behind only marijuana. In 2010, the Substance Abuse and Mental Health Services Administration reported that the proportion of all substance abuse treatment admissions aged 12 or older that reported any pain reliever abuse increased more than fourfold from 1998 to 2008.[2] In terms of the economic costs, a study by the University of Washington estimated the cost of the abuse of prescription pain relievers in 2006 to be $53.4 billion.[3]

Controlled substances can be diverted in many different ways, and new methods continue to evolve over time. Diversion can occur as a result of illegal or improper prescribing, prescription forgery, pharmacy thefts, or "doctor shopping" where an individual—who may or may not have legitimate medical needs—goes to several doctors to obtain a prescription from each doctor. Diversion can also occur through illegal sales of controlled substances, such as drugs sold by physicians, patients, or pharmacists, as well as individuals obtaining these substances without a valid prescription through Internet pharmacies or pain clinics.[4] According to DEA, from fiscal years 2006 through 2009, rogue Internet pharmacies were a major source of this problem, where individuals could obtain controlled substances through Internet pharmacies without establishing a legitimate doctor/patient relationship. Following increased enforcement actions against rogue Internet pharmacies, another source emerged in the form of rogue pain clinics where prescriptions for controlled substances could similarly be obtained without a legitimate medical need. These pain clinics have proliferated in states such as Florida and Texas.

Controlled substance diversion poses a unique challenge because of the need to balance prevention, education, and enforcement with the need for legitimate access. Within the Drug Enforcement Administration (DEA), the Office of Diversion Control is directly responsible for enforcing the provisions of the CSA as they pertain to ensuring the availability of substances such as prescription drugs and listed chemicals for legitimate uses while preventing their diversion. As part of the provisions to control access to such substances, the CSA requires businesses, entities, or individuals that import, export, manufacture, distribute, dispense, conduct research with respect to, or administer controlled substances to register with the DEA. One of the key activities of the Office of Diversion Control is to conduct investigations—regulatory investigations to monitor compliance of the registrants with the CSA and its implementing regulations, and criminal investigations into instances of potential criminal diversion.

Because of the rising diversion and illicit use of controlled prescription drugs, you asked us to review DEA's management of its diversion control investigations to combat this problem.[5] Specifically, this report answers the following questions:

1) How does DEA manage its investigation efforts to address the growing and evolving nature of prescription drug diversion?
2) How does DEA help ensure that policies and procedures are followed for diversion investigations and to what extent does it determine the results of its efforts on the diversion problem?

To address the first objective, we reviewed DEA policies and procedures on how DEA carries out its investigative responsibilities, including program documents such as DEA's current strategic plan and budget justification submissions for fiscal years 2008 to 2012.[6] We also analyzed DEA data for fiscal years 2007 to 2010 on case volumes for investigations and data on number of personnel working on DEA's Tactical Diversion Squads (squads).[7] We reviewed information from agency officials regarding the data and the systems and procedures used to maintain it. From this review we determined that the data were sufficiently reliable for the purposes of this report. We also interviewed DEA program officials involved in overseeing and managing diversion control investigations and program officials involved in diversion investigations at 5 of DEA's 21 field divisions. These included Seattle, Washington; Houston, Texas; Miami, Florida; Washington, D.C.; and Atlanta, Georgia. As part of these interviews, we obtained DEA program officials' perspectives on how they carry out diversion investigations and how they work with other federal, state, and local agencies, as well as registrants in carrying out investigatory activities. These field divisions were selected on the basis of a mix of criteria such as the range of the highest volumes of regulatory and criminal cases and civil penalties; geographic diversity; and other considerations. Within each field division, we also contacted and interviewed officials of state boards of pharmacy and medicine to obtain information on how DEA coordinates with their agencies. In order to better understand how DEA is using its squads to respond to criminal diversion, we interviewed DEA officials and officials from state and local agencies participating in the squads to obtain information on how criminal diversion investigations are carried out and how DEA coordinates those investigations. The 10 squads selected for these interviews were Baltimore, Maryland; Worcester, Massachusetts; Houston, Texas; Kansas City, Missouri; Miami, Florida; New Orleans, Louisiana; Oakland, California; Seattle, Washington; Tampa, Florida; and Washington, D.C., and were chosen based on a mix of criteria such as the range of the highest volume of cases handled, length of time in operation, and the participation of state and local agencies. Our results are not generalizable across all field divisions or squads but provide a broad overview and understanding of diversion investigations, as well as how DEA has managed these investigations and coordinates with other non-DEA partners. We also interviewed officials with associations representing pharmacies and distributors, as well as pharmacies and distributors identified by these associations, to obtain regulated industry's perspective on how DEA carries out its regulatory responsibilities and interacts with this industry. The information we obtained from interviewing officials with these associations as well as officials with pharmacies and distributors that were identified by the associations, cannot be generalized across the entire population of pharmacy and distributor operators. However, the information gathered in these interviews provided us with perspectives from regulated industry on how DEA has implemented its diversion control efforts and how it interacts with industry in monitoring compliance with the CSA.

To address the second objective, we compared criteria in *Standards for Internal Control in the Federal Government* to (1) DEA's control activities related to human capital management and (2) DEA's monitoring mechanisms to identify what actions it has taken to ensure its employees are informed and follow required policies and procedures.[8] We also reviewed DEA policies and procedures in its manuals for Diversion Investigators and Special Agents, as well as documents related to DEA training courses conducted for program personnel to determine DEA's efforts to ensure its employees have the required knowledge to conduct diversion investigations. We reviewed the most recent on-site internal inspection reports for each of DEA's 21 field divisions, ranging from fiscal years 2005 to 2010 to determine what issues, if any, were identified with respect to diversion investigations.[9] At headquarters, we interviewed DEA program officials in the Office of Training, Office of Inspections, and the Regulatory Section. Our purpose was to determine what actions they take to train employees on required policies and procedures and conduct reviews of employee work products. We also reviewed DEA's Strategic Plan Fiscal Years 2009-2014 to identify DEA's plans for ongoing monitoring efforts. To determine how DEA measures the results of its efforts against the diversion problem, we reviewed DEA's Strategic Plan Fiscal Years 2009-2014, as well as the corresponding performance measures DEA has designated for the diversion control program as reported in its budget justifications for fiscal years 2008 through 2012. We compared DEA's identified performance measures with best practices for performance measurement identified in our previous guidance and work regarding the implementation of the Government Performance and Results Act to determine the extent to which the measures could be used to demonstrate program results.[10] We also interviewed DEA officials within the Office of Diversion Control and the Office of Resource Management to determine how they use these measures, and what plans, among other things, they had to evaluate the usefulness of the measures as indicators to track results towards the program's overall performance goal of reducing the diversion of licit drugs.

We conducted this performance audit from May 2010 through August 2011 in accordance with generally accepted government auditing standards. Those standards require that we plan and perform the audit to obtain sufficient, appropriate evidence to provide a reasonable basis for our findings and conclusions based on our audit objectives. We believe that the evidence obtained provides a reasonable basis for our findings and conclusions based on our audit objectives.

BACKGROUND

The CSA and DEA's Office of Diversion Control

The CSA places various plants, drugs, and chemicals such as narcotics, stimulants, depressants, hallucinogens, and anabolic steroids, into one of five schedules based on the substance's medical use or lack thereof, potential for abuse, and safety or potential for dependence.[11]

The act requires persons who handle controlled substances and/or listed chemicals (such as manufacturers, wholesale distributors, physicians who dispense controlled substances, hospitals, pharmacies, importers/exporters, and scientific researchers) to register with the DEA. This agency, by delegation from the U.S. Attorney General, is responsible for administering and enforcing the CSA and its implementing regulations.

Through its Office of Diversion Control, DEA administers the Diversion Control Program whose mission is to prevent, detect, and investigate the diversion of controlled pharmaceuticals and listed chemicals into the illicit market, while ensuring an adequate and uninterrupted supply for legitimate needs. In addition to conducting investigations, the office conducts a variety of activities such as the establishment of production quotas, drafting and promulgating regulations for handling controlled substances, regulating handlers of controlled substances, and monitoring and tracking the production and distribution of certain controlled substances, among other things.

To carry out this mission, the Office of Diversion Control is authorized approximately 1,300 full-time equivalent positions and a budget of approximately $292 million. The program is funded through the Diversion Control Fee Account, which consists of registration fees paid by registrants.

DEA Registers Entities Authorized to Handle Controlled Substances

As required by the CSA, businesses, individuals, or entities that import, export, manufacture, distribute, dispense, conduct research with respect to controlled substances and/or listed chemicals must register with the DEA.

DEA has more than 1.3 million individuals and companies that are registered to handle controlled substances or regulated chemicals. These registrants include manufacturers, distributors, and importers/exporters of controlled substances or medications; pharmacies, hospitals, narcotic treatment programs, and clinics that dispense controlled medications; practitioners who prescribe and administer or dispense controlled medications; and researchers who use controlled substances or medications in their research or analyses (see table 1.)

Schedules of controlled substances

Controlled substances are classified into five schedules on the basis of their currently accepted medical use and potential for abuse and dependence:

- Schedule I substances have no currently accepted medical uses and have a high potential for abuse. Examples: heroin and marijuana.
- Schedule II substances have currently accepted medical uses but also have high potential for abuse that may lead to severe psychological or physical dependence. Examples: oxycodone and (methylphenidate) Ritalin.
- Schedule III substances have currently accepted medical uses and a potential for abuse which may lead to moderate or low physical dependence or high psychological dependence. Examples: anabolic steroids, codeine, and hydrocodone in combination with aspirin or acetaminophen.
- Schedule IV substances have currently accepted medical uses and a low potential for abuse which may lead to limited physical or psychological dependence. Examples: anti-anxiety medications diazepam (Valium) and alprazolam (Xanax).
- Schedule V substances have currently accepted medical uses and a low potential for abuse which may lead to limited physical or psychological dependence. Example: cough syrup preparations with codeine.

All drugs but those in Schedule I are legally available with a prescription.

Sources: 21 U.S.C. § 812; GAO.

Table 1. DEA Registrants, by Type, as of May 2011

Registrant type	Number of registrant type	Percent of total registrant population
Practitioner	1,103,159	79.46%
Mid-Level Practitioner	188,577	13.58%
Retail Pharmacy	66,829	4.81%
Hospital/Clinic	15,735	1.13%
Researcher	9,036	0.65%
Analytical Labs	1,483	0.11%
Narcotic Treatment Program	1,259	0.09%
Distributor	793	0.06%
Manufacturer	526	0.04%
Teaching Institute	348	0.03%
Exporter	228	0.02%
Importer	206	0.01%
Reverse Distributor[a]	59	<0.01%
Total	1,388,238	100.00%

Source: DEA.

Notes:

[a] A reverse distributor is a registrant who receives controlled substances acquired from another DEA registrant for the purpose of returning unwanted, unusable, or outdated controlled substances to the manufacturer or the manufacturer's agent, or processes such substances or arranges for processing such substances for disposal.

In order to maintain their registration, DEA registrants must comply with a variety of regulatory requirements imposed by the CSA and its implementing regulations. Examples of these regulatory requirements include:

- *Recordkeeping:* A registrant must keep accurate records and maintain detailed inventories of controlled substances in compliance with applicable federal and state laws. For example, the registrant must maintain accurate records of each substance manufactured, received, sold, delivered, or otherwise disposed of by the registrant.
- *Reporting:* Manufacturers and distributors must report acquisition or distribution transactions of certain controlled substances, such as Schedule I and II drugs and Schedule III narcotics, to DEA through the Automated Reports and Consolidated Orders System (ARCOS). ARCOS is an automated reporting system to monitor the flow of controlled substances from their point of manufacture to the point of sale or distribution at the dispensing/retail level such as hospitals,

retail pharmacies, practitioners, midlevel practitioners, and teaching institutions. Manufacturing transactions of Schedule I and II controlled substances, as well as Schedule III and IV narcotics, among others are also covered by the ARCOS reporting requirements.

- *Dispensing of controlled substances:* The CSA provides special requirements for licensed practitioners and pharmacists who dispense controlled substances in Schedules II-V to patients. For example, a prescription for a controlled substance must be "issued for a legitimate medical purpose by an individual practitioner acting in the usual course of his professional practice." Accordingly, practitioners also have a responsibility to ensure that the controlled substance is properly prescribed and dispensed while a corresponding responsibility exists with the pharmacist filling the prescription.
- *Security of controlled substances:* For the purposes of ensuring the secure storage and distribution of controlled substances, all registrants must "provide effective controls and procedures to guard against theft and diversion of controlled substances."

  Among other things, DEA regulations also detail specific security requirements for the different types of applicants and registrants. For example, nonpractitioners (i.e., manufacturers, distributors, and narcotic treatment programs) are required to store Schedule I and II substances in electronically monitored safes, steel cabinets, or vaults that meet or exceed certain specifications.

  Licensed practitioners must store controlled substances in a "securely locked, substantially constructed cabinet" and must notify DEA of the theft or significant loss of any controlled substances.

DEA Investigations to Monitor and Enforce CSA Compliance

To achieve its mission, DEA monitors and enforces compliance with the CSA through three types of investigations—regulatory, complaint, and criminal:

- **Regulatory Investigations:** DEA conducts scheduled investigations or inspections (depending on the registrants, the frequency of the scheduled investigations can range from every 3 years to every 5 years) of wholesale registrants who include manufacturers, distributors, importer/exporters, and narcotic treatment programs as well as other registrants such as researchers, analytical labs, and teaching institutions, among others. Retail level registrants such as pharmacies and physicians—with the exception of physicians permitted to treat narcotic dependence—do not receive regulatory investigations by the DEA. These registrants are regularly investigated by the states in which they conduct business. According to DEA officials, they focus their efforts related to regulatory investigations on the wholesale registrants because such registrants are the sources of supply to criminal schemes such as rogue pharmacies and pill mills. To conduct these investigations, DEA Diversion Investigators arrive at the registrant unannounced and inspect and verify the registrant's records, take a physical inventory of the registrant's controlled substances, and inspect any other items necessary to verify the registrant's compliance with the CSA and its implementing regulations. If deficiencies are found during the investigation, DEA may work with the registrant to correct the deficiencies. DEA may also take administrative, civil, or criminal action against the registrant depending on the type, severity, and frequency of the deficiencies found.

- **Complaint Investigations:** Complaint investigations are investigations that are started on the basis of information or a tip provided to DEA or state regulators, or other information DEA has regarding purchases or losses of controlled substances.
  The origin of the information could be from any number of sources, such as a state or local official or citizen that saw something suspicious, employees of a registrant, the identification of unusual purchasing trends by a registrant such as a pharmacy tracked by DEA through its ARCOS, or a report of a loss of controlled substances by a registrant. Diversion Investigators conduct preliminary investigative work to determine whether the information is valid and warrants a full investigation. Depending on the outcome of the preliminary complaint investigation, DEA determines whether the investigation will be handled as a regulatory noncompliance issue, a criminal case, or a dismissal.
- **Criminal Investigations**: DEA also conducts investigations into criminal activities involving diversion of controlled substances. Criminal diversion may involve DEA registrants such as pharmacies and practitioners and nonregistrants such as pharmacy burglars or doctor shoppers, among others.

Penalties for diversion of controlled substances

DEA can initiate a variety of actions for violations of the CSA or its implementing regulations. The type(s) of action taken is typically driven by the severity of the offense(s) and whether or not a registrant was the subject of any previous actions. The following is a partial listing of potential actions DEA can take against a registrant or diverter:

- Administrative actions are handled primarily by DEA and can include (1) a letter of admonition to advise the registrant of any violations; (2) an order to show cause which initiates revocation or suspension of a DEA registration; and (3) an immediate suspension order against the registrant if there is a finding of imminent threat to public health or safety.
- Civil penalties are typically coordinated with an Assistant United States Attorney or in some instances the local district attorney. Civil violations are typically recordkeeping violations involving controlled substances or listed chemicals. Penalties for civil actions generally include monetary fines.
- Criminal prosecutions are coordinated with an Assistant United States Attorney or local district attorney. Criminal violations include offenses such as the illegal distribution of controlled substances and other related offenses such as health care fraud, tax evasion, and money laundering. Criminal penalties generally include incarceration and fines.

Source: DEA.

Within its 21 field divisions, DEA utilizes a variety of personnel to carry out these investigative responsibilities:

- *Diversion Investigators* conduct investigations of regulatory, civil, and criminal issues pertaining to DEA registrants. The investigators do not have law enforcement authority and cannot perform law enforcement functions such as making arrests and conducting surveillance.
- *Special Agents* conduct diversion investigations and assist Diversion Investigators by performing law enforcement functions such as serving search warrants and making arrests.

- *Diversion Program Managers* oversee diversion control activities in their field division.
- *Special Agents-in-Charge* manage the activities of the DEA field division including diversion control activities.
- *Assistant Special Agents-in-Charge* assist the Special Agents-in-Charge in managing activities of the field division including diversion control activities.

DEA Has Expanded Its Resources and Targeted Its Investigation Strategies to Respond to Rising Criminal Diversion and Growing Registrant Population

To respond to the increasing rate of criminal diversion and a growing registrant population, DEA has expanded its resources and targeted investigation strategies in ways to collaborate with state and local entities and enhance the effectiveness of its Diversion Control Program. Specifically, DEA has expanded its use of Tactical Diversion Squads, which work with DEA's state, local, and other federal partners, to maximize resources and improve efforts to investigate, disrupt, and dismantle individuals or organizations involved in diversion schemes related to controlled substances and listed chemicals. DEA has also renewed its focus on regulatory oversight of the more than 1.3 million DEA registrants to ensure registrants comply with the CSA and implementing regulations. DEA accomplished this by increasing the frequency of scheduled investigations of DEA registrants that are registered to handle controlled prescription drugs.

Tactical Diversion Squad Expansion Provides Additional Resources and Facilitates Coordination and Information Sharing for Criminal Investigations

To help respond to the ever-changing methods of criminal diversion such as rogue pain clinics and rogue Internet pharmacy schemes, in October 2008 the DEA acting Administrator authorized the expansion of squads devoted to addressing criminal diversion of controlled substances and listed chemicals across the United States. DEA has historically utilized these squads, called

Tactical Diversion Squads (squads), as a collaborative mechanism to address the criminal diversion of controlled substances. The squads are teams of DEA diversion personnel (such as Special Agents and Diversion Investigators), as well as state and local law enforcement personnel (task force officers) whose mission is to detect, investigate, and refer for prosecution, violators of federal and state statutes pertaining to diversion. They also develop investigative leads from information and intelligence obtained from participating agencies, undercover operations, and the use of informants. This multiagency effort helps coordinate the investigative activities of the participating agencies. According to DEA, the squads also allow DEA to provide manpower for diversion investigations at reduced costs to DEA because task force officer positions are less expensive than Special Agents or Diversion Investigators. For example, DEA compensates state and local Tactical Diversion Squad task force officers for overtime, use of a vehicle, equipment, and diversion training, while the parent agencies are responsible for their task force officers' salary and benefits.

This expansion resulted in a significant increase in the number of Special Agents and task force officers for criminal diversion investigations. At the time the expansion was authorized, DEA had 5 squads in operation which, according to DEA officials, were authorized 5 Special Agents, 12 Diversion Investigators, and 27 task force officers. With existing positions and funding previously authorized and agreements with state and local law enforcement partners in place, DEA has since established 35 additional squads across the United States (see fig. 1) increasing the total number of Special Agents, Diversion Investigators, and task force officers working on all the squads to a total of 141, 54, and 301, respectively.[12] With the increase in squads, DEA has been able to perform more criminal investigations each year. For example, DEA was able to increase the number of criminal investigations initiated from 1,571 in fiscal year 2009 to 1,904 in fiscal year 2010, an increase of 21 percent. According to the Executive Assistant to the Deputy Assistant Administrator for Diversion Control, they plan to add 16 more squads between fiscal years 2011 and 2013 and eventually have at least 63 squads across the country, depending on the need for the squads and availability of resources. With the further expansion of these squads, DEA officials stated that they expect to continue to be able to conduct more criminal diversion investigations each year. To staff these additional squads, DEA requested an additional 60 Special Agent, 37 Diversion Investigator, and 64 task force officer positions for fiscal year 2011, and an additional 50 Special Agent, 16 Diversion Investigator, and 64 task force officer positions for fiscal year 2012. Because the Diversion Control program is funded through its fee account, DEA officials noted that such increases in personnel are contingent on the revision of the schedule of fees charged registrants, which is currently underway.[13] They anticipate beginning to collect fees under the revised fee schedule in fiscal year 2012. DEA's current annual registrant fees range from $184 to $2,293.[14] The last time DEA revised its fees was in 2006.

Coordination with state partners: Prescription Drug Monitoring Programs

State Prescription Drug Monitoring Programs (PDMPs) provide data and analysis to state law enforcement and regulatory agencies to assist in identifying activities potentially related to the illegal prescribing, dispensing, and procuring of controlled substances. The PDMP can be designed to identify possible abusers or diverters by tracking the volume and frequency of prescriptions. As of June 2011, 35 states have operational PDMPs that have the capability to receive and distribute controlled substance prescription information to authorized users. As the PDMP is a state program, DEA does not have a role in its implementation or operation. However, DEA can access PDMP data for use in squad investigations. In 2002, we reported that states with PDMPs experienced considerable reductions in the time and effort required to investigate drug diversion cases (see GAO-02-634).

Sources: GAO; DEA.

Coordinating with state and local law enforcement has been beneficial to the squads in investigating diversion. According to squad participants in 6 of the 10 squads we contacted, state and local law enforcement's participation is critical because they are familiar with the local communities they patrol and are able to bring information from their communities to the investigations.[15] At the same time, participating in the squad has enabled local law enforcement agencies to carry out more complex investigations into diversion within their localities. For example, although some local law enforcement agencies had conducted investigations of lower level diverters such as doctor shoppers prior to the establishment of squads, they did not have the resources on their own to carry out the longer, more complex investigations required for targeting higher level diverters such as physicians and their clinics. DEA officials noted that state and local agencies also lack the administrative authorities DEA has to take action against a DEA registrant when necessary. The squad provided a means for state and local law enforcement to collectively pool their resources with DEA to investigate higher level diverters.

Source: GAO analysis of DEA data; Copyright © Corel Corp. All rights reserved (map).

Figure 1. Location of the 40 Tactical Diversion Squads.

Based on feedback from squad participants and DEA officials we interviewed, coordination and information sharing within the squads were reported as excellent and an improvement over presquad times. According to DEA and local officials we interviewed, the establishment of the squads has been a means to improve communication, coordination, and simplify information sharing as the squads have become the clearinghouse for diversion-related investigative information. As a result, information is now shared more rapidly and broadly between law enforcement agencies, according to these officials we interviewed. These squads have also become an important deconfliction mechanism for law enforcement agencies regarding the diversion cases they are working or information they receive from other sources. For example, one local law enforcement official with a task force officer on a squad stated that all leads his department receives for potential diversion investigations are first referred to the squad to determine whether there are any links to ongoing squad investigations or if the lead would be an appropriate target for it to take on as a new investigation.

Example of diversion of controlled substances—Illegal pain clinics

States such as Florida have experienced significant diversion problems through illegal pain clinics. According to DEA officials, Florida physicians order the majority of oxycodone compared to the rest of the country. In 2010, Florida dispensing physicians ordered over 41 million dosage units of oxycodone, while the rest of the country ordered a total of 4 million dosage units. Some of these physicians are reported to have links to illegal pain clinics where they either dispensed or wrote prescriptions that were not for legitimate medical purposes. Individuals from other states would come to Florida to visit the clinics to obtain controlled substances for abuse or resale. Florida recently enacted legislation to address these clinics. Similarly, Texas and Louisiana have experienced problems with illegal pain clinics and also enacted legislation to address this roblem. Among other things, the legislation for these states requires pain clinics to be owned and operated by licensed physicians with no previous medical board action, and to register with state regulators.

Sources: DEA, Federation of State Medical Boards, and National Drug Intelligence Center (data); Edward Linsmier/St. Petersburg Times (image).

The picture shows a line up of individuals detained after a law enforcement raid of a Florida pain clinic.

Federal agencies such as the Federal Bureau of Investigation (FBI), the U.S. Department of Health and Human Services (HHS), and the Internal Revenue Service (IRS) may also be involved in the squads' criminal investigations depending on the case and if their expertise is needed. For example, FBI agents will generally join a squad's investigation if fraud is involved; HHS investigators may become involved in investigations related to health care fraud; and IRS agents may assist in investigations involving tax evasion and money laundering. In March 2011, for example, the DEA in conjunction with the FBI and HHS, among other agencies, concluded an investigation into a Detroit physician for unlawfully distributing controlled substances, including the Schedule II controlled substance OxyContin (oxycodone), and fraudulently billing Medicare.

Tactical Diversion Squad investigation: Operation Pill Nation

To deal with criminal diversion, DEA through its Tactical Diversion Squads worked with federal, state, and local law enforcement partners to conduct criminal investigations. As an example of collaborative actions to address criminal diversion, the Miami Tactical Diversion Squad and its law enforcement partners are conducting an investigative effort called Operation Pill Nation. This operation involved the mobilization of 11 squads from across the United States to coordinate with the Miami Tactical Diversion Squad in investigating illegal pain clinics. As of April 2011, DEA reported that the investigation resulted in the closure of 38 clinics, the arrest of 32 individuals including 12 physicians, the seizure of more than $16.4 million in assets, and the surrender of 83 DEA registrations.

Source: DEA.

Exotic cars seized during Operation Pill Nation.

According to DEA, a conviction of this offense carries a maximum of 20 years in prison, a fine of $1 million, or both. In another example, according to DEA squad officials, DEA, FBI, and IRS, among others, conducted a joint criminal investigation into a Texas business owner's rogue Internet pharmacy scheme. The investigation resulted in a guilty plea to several offenses including unlawfully distributing controlled substances, money laundering, and fraudulently billing healthcare providers, among other offenses. According to DEA officials, joint investigations with other federal agencies are very helpful for the squad in advancing the investigation because the other federal agencies bring specific subject matter expertise in areas that DEA staff do not have.

DEA Has Significantly Increased the Number of Regulatory Investigations to Help Ensure Growing Registrant Population Complies with CSA

In addition to the expansion of the squads in October 2008, the DEA acting Administrator also called for an enhanced focus on DEA's regulatory oversight aimed at ensuring that the more than 1.3 million DEA registrants comply with the CSA and its implementing regulations. According to DEA, the overall registrant population tends to grow at a rate of 2 to 2.5 percent annually; however, registrants such as Drug Addiction Treatment Act[16] waived physicians (DWPs) have grown faster. For example, from fiscal year 2002 to fiscal year 2010 the number of DEA registered DWPs increased from 1,451 to 19,211, an increase of about 1,300 percent. DWPs are physicians who dispense or prescribe Federal Food and Drug Administration approved buprenorphine products for treatment of narcotic addiction/dependence on an outpatient basis. In an effort to help meet the demand for this specialty, the Drug Addiction Treatment Act of 2000 waived the requirement for qualified physicians to obtain a separate DEA registration as a Narcotic Treatment Program in order to provide medication-assisted chemical substance therapy.[17] With the enactment of the act, the Substance Abuse and Mental Health Services Administration within HHS aggressively pursued training for interested physicians to help meet this demand. As a result, there was a significant increase in the number of physicians who registered with DEA as DWPs. In response to this growing registrant population, DEA increased the frequency of scheduled investigations of DWPs as part of the enhanced regulatory oversight called for by the acting Administrator. For example, in October 2008, DEA decided to move towards conducting regulatory investigations of all DWPs every 5 years to monitor for compliance. Previously DEA was conducting regulatory investigations of only one DWP in each of its 21 Field Divisions annually, a rate that, given the growth of that registrant type, would have taken decades for DEA to investigate all registered DWPs, according to the Executive Assistant to the Deputy Assistant

Administrator for the Diversion Control Program. According to DEA's Chief of the Regulatory Section, the decision to increase the rate for conducting regulatory investigations of DWPs was also due, in part, to some DWPs not complying with regulatory requirements relating to recordkeeping and the loss of controlled substances used to treat patients.

DEA also increased the frequency of regulatory investigations for other registrant types as well, such as registrants involved in the manufacture and distribution of drugs (from once every 5 years to once every 3 years), and chemicals (from once every 3 years to once every 2 years).[18] For some registrant types that had not previously been subject to regulatory investigation, such as researchers, analytical labs, and teaching institutions, DEA required that regulatory investigations be conducted once every 5 years. According to DEA's Chief of the Regulatory Section, the increase in the frequency of regulatory investigations for some registrant types was also due to the registrants' noncompliance with the CSA and DEA's implementing regulations. For example, some distributors did not report suspicious orders for controlled substances to DEA, as required by regulation.[19] Reflecting the changes in requirements for regulatory investigations, DEA more than tripled the number of regulatory investigations from 1,173 in fiscal year 2009 to 3,731 in fiscal year 2010 (see fig. 2 below).

According to the Executive Assistant to the Deputy Assistant Administrator for Diversion Control, DEA was able to increase its regulatory investigations primarily by using the squads to free up Diversion Investigator resources that had previously been working both criminal and regulatory cases and DEA plans to hire additional diversion staff in the future to conduct investigations. To keep up with the level of regulatory investigations to be completed in the future, DEA plans to hire additional staff. For example, for fiscal year 2011 DEA requested 60 Diversion Investigator positions and for fiscal year 2012 requested an additional 50 Diversion Investigator positions, pending completion of the revision of the schedule of fees charged registrants, which must provide the funding necessary to fill those positions.[20] According to DEA officials, of the 60 Diversion Investigator positions requested for fiscal year 2011, 23 were requested to support regulatory activities while 37 were to support the squads; for fiscal year 2012, of the 50 Diversion Investigator positions requested, 34 were for regulatory activities and 16 for support of the squads.

Source: GAO analysis of DEA data.

Figure 2. Number of Regulatory Investigations Initiated by DEA Diversion Control, by Fiscal Year.

In addition to conducting regulatory investigations, DEA has also actively engaged registrants and their industry associations to help the registrants understand current trends in diversion and the regulatory obligations they must demonstrate that they have fulfilled during regulatory investigations. For example, DEA periodically hosts conferences for the chemical and pharmaceutical industries to share information on current trends, issues, federal laws, and regulations, and to discuss practices to prevent diversion. Industry associations reported that DEA also attends industry-sponsored conferences and shares useful information and guidance. In addition, regulated industry reported that DEA provides information to registrants on DEA's Web site as well as through policy letters and correspondence. According to DEA officials, they also speak at conferences such as the National Association of Boards of Pharmacy, the American Society of Interventional Pain Physicians, pharmacy schools, and other industry venues.

Furthermore, DEA has conducted other targeted outreach efforts to specific registrant types to inform them of specific regulatory responsibilities or help them prepare for regulatory investigations:

- In 2005 DEA established an initiative to better inform wholesale distributors of controlled substances of their responsibilities under the CSA to report suspicious orders from pharmacies that are possibly filling invalid prescriptions. As part of this initiative, DEA created a presentation explaining the laws, regulations, and DEA policies. The presentation provided examples of Internet pharmacies and rogue pain clinics as well as their purchase patterns and methods of operation. The presentation was designed to emphasize the need for wholesalers to utilize due diligence, and when appropriate, stop supplying retail outlets with controlled substances where diversion is occurring. From August 2005 through March 2011, DEA reported briefing 74 corporations concerning illegal Internet pharmacy operations and rogue pain clinics. Since the launch of the program, DEA reports that distributors have voluntarily stopped selling or restricted sales of controlled substances to approximately 1,390 customers believed to be placing suspicious orders for such substances.
- During 2009 and 2010, DEA's Office of Diversion Control officials met with a number of DWPs and industry associations that represent DWPs to inform them about the regulatory investigation process and regulatory requirements. They discussed recordkeeping and the security of controlled substances, among other items, that DWPs must meet to comply with the CSA and its implementing regulations.

DEA's Internal Controls Help to Ensure the Quality of Investigations, but DEA Could Enhance Efforts to Measure Program Results

DEA helps to ensure the quality of its diversion control investigations through the use of internal controls, but could enhance its efforts to measure the results of its Diversion Control Program. To ensure that Diversion Investigators and Special Agents have the necessary skills to carry out their responsibilities and that DEA monitors the results of its employee guidance and training, DEA has established internal control activities, which are consistent with *Standards for Internal Control in the Federal Government.* DEA has established performance measures to assess and report on its progress toward meeting its performance goal of reducing the diversion of licit drugs, but could reassess the measures to identify ways to better capture and report on the results of DEA's investigations.

DEA's Efforts to Ensure Its Staff Have the Necessary Guidance, Training, and Oversight Are Consistent with Internal Control Standards

Diversion investigations are the primary means DEA uses to monitor registrant compliance with the CSA and to identify diversion activities. As such, it is important that the employees responsible for conducting investigations—Diversion Investigators and Special Agents—have the necessary skills to carry out their responsibilities and that DEA management monitors the results of its investigative efforts. To accomplish this, DEA has established internal control activities related to guidance, training, and monitoring. Given DEA's increased focus on regulatory and criminal investigations in response to growing and evolving diversion, these internal controls help to provide reasonable assurance that investigators and agents have the necessary skill levels to meet existing program requirements for diversion investigations and changing organizational priorities as new trends in diversion emerge.

DEA Guidance and Training Provide Investigators Tools Needed for Investigations

DEA has established internal control activities related to guidance and training such as program policy and procedures manuals and diversion investigation courses. These efforts are consistent with *Standards for Internal Control in the Federal Government*, which state that agency management should help to ensure it has a workforce that has the required skills that match those necessary to achieve organizational goals. Specifically, DEA provides guidance in the form of manuals to its Diversion Investigators and Special Agents on the policies and procedures they are to follow in conducting diversion investigations. DEA officials told us that they use this guidance for conducting diversion investigations and reviewing employee work products. The Diversion Investigator Manual describes and explains the policies and procedures for Diversion Investigators in carrying out their regulatory and investigative responsibilities, the processes for conducting diversion investigations, and the procedures for developing investigative reports. The Special Agent Manual describes and explains the responsibilities of Special Agents in diversion investigations.[21]

In order to familiarize employees with the process for conducting diversion investigations and related policies and procedures, DEA requires basic training for new employees and offers advanced and supplemental training courses to existing personnel within the Diversion Control Program to help them maintain the knowledge and skills necessary to conduct diversion investigations. Specifically, DEA's Office of Training provides a 12-week basic course to newly hired Diversion Investigator personnel, which includes techniques for diversion investigations among other relevant subjects, to help ensure that they have the required skills for performing investigator responsibilities.[22] The training is provided through a combination of in-classroom lessons and practical application; direct observation; and instructor-to-trainee feedback. Course trainees must maintain an 80 percent average on exams and simulated on-site investigations in order to pass the course and be certified as a Diversion Investigator. After the completion of basic training, the investigators enter into duty under a 1-year probationary period with a midpoint review provided after 6 months of duty. In addition, according to DEA officials we spoke with, group supervisors may go on-site with newly hired employees to help ensure that they are familiar with the requirements of investigations.

DEA also requires its Diversion Investigators to complete an advanced (or in-service refresher) training course every 2 years to help ensure their investigative skills and knowledge remain current. The advanced training course is a 1-week course that focuses on current legal issues in diversion, recent updates to DEA program policies and technology, investigative techniques, and any other new initiatives or programs that DEA has incorporated as part of the diversion control program within the previous 2 years. Officials in DEA's Office of Training told us that the topics that are covered during the advanced training course are identified through a biannual survey of Diversion Investigators and group supervisors to find out what issues they are facing in their work or what additional guidance is needed. DEA's efforts to help ensure Diversion Investigators maintain their investigative skills and are informed of new program initiatives and program policy changes are consistent with federal internal controls standards which state that training should be aimed at developing and retaining employee skill levels to meet changing organizational needs.

Beyond the required basic and advanced training courses, Diversion Investigators and supervisors may take additional courses in other relevant subject matter areas as time, resources, and needs permit. For example, officials in DEA's Office of Training told us that they offer specialized courses on specific issues related to diversion control investigations such as interviewing techniques, chemical investigations, techniques for financial investigations, and asset forfeiture, among others. Furthermore, the Diversion Control Program's field divisions may occasionally sponsor supplemental training for personnel that they determine would be beneficial. Typically, such training is shorter in duration and narrowly focused on topics such as report writing, interviewing techniques, or legal or investigative issues specific to that division.

Group supervisors of Diversion Investigators also receive supervisory training to help ensure that they have the requisite knowledge to perform their supervisory responsibilities, including those responsibilities related to reviewing the work of Diversion Investigators. Specifically, when first promoted, supervisors attend a supervisory institute to learn their new roles and responsibilities as supervisors as well as receive training in management and leadership techniques. Group supervisors also have electronic access to PowerPoint presentations, handouts, and administrative manuals to help guide them in carrying out these responsibilities once they return to duty. As with the Diversion Investigators, supervisors also receive a 1-week advanced supervisor refresher course every 2 years.

Special Agents assigned to the Diversion Control Program are also provided training related to conducting criminal diversion investigations. The training for Special Agents includes a 1-week course to provide them with an in-depth understanding of criminal diversion investigations and includes instruction on methods of diversion, Internet investigations, and the investigative techniques to develop criminal investigations, among other issue areas related to diversion control.

Furthermore, DEA's Office of Diversion Control recently developed and implemented a new training curriculum designed to retrain and retool all Diversion Investigators. According to DEA officials, as the reorganization of the diversion program required Diversion Investigators to conduct more regulatory investigations than previously, the retraining was developed to refresh the investigators' skills and abilities for conducting the investigations. DEA officials reported that as of December 2010, all Diversion Investigators completed this training. These efforts are consistent with federal internal control standards which provide that training should help to retain employee skill levels in order to meet changes in organizational needs.

To assess the effectiveness of its training courses, officials in DEA's Office of Training stated that they obtain student feedback on a training course evaluation form at the conclusion of each training course. Additionally, DEA training officials review the curriculum for basic Diversion Investigator training every 3 years using feedback from students and input from a training working group comprised of Diversion Investigators and group supervisors to ensure that the material being presented is relevant and up to date. DEA officials also reported that the Office of Training is in constant communication with diversion management staff at headquarters and in the field to ensure that the training curriculums include updated policies relating to diversion operations.

DEA's Monitoring Process Did Not Identify Widespread or Systematic Problems with the Quality of Investigations

As DEA continues to enhance its diversion control efforts, it is important that it has controls in place to review the quality of its diversion investigations and to test the effectiveness of its review process in order to readily identify and resolve deficiencies related to its key compliance activity. Standards for internal control in the federal government provide that internal control monitoring should assess the quality of performance over time and ensure that findings of audits and other reviews are promptly resolved. DEA's internal control monitoring activities collectively are consistent with these standards, which also state that internal controls should generally be designed to assure that ongoing monitoring occurs in the normal course of operations. Internal control monitoring includes regular management and supervisory activities among other activities and is performed continually. DEA has implemented a multilayered approach to monitor the work of its Diversion Control Program personnel to help ensure that they are following policies and procedures for diversion investigations. The monitoring process includes direct supervisory review, self-inspection/peer review, and on-site internal inspection. Additionally, DEA assesses the effectiveness of its monitoring process by reviewing the results of inspections conducted as a part of the overall program evaluation responsibilities of DEA's Office of Inspections (IN) and deter-mining actions necessary for improvement and additional employee training needs. Furthermore, DEA's 2009-2014 Strategic Plan reflects that the agency plans to use the Office of Inspections to help ensure effective and efficient program oversight through its on-site inspections.

DEA field division supervisory officials reported that they directly review employee work products to assess the extent to which employees are following required policies and procedures for diversion investigations. Specifically, these supervisory officials review reports and active case files submitted by their employees for completeness, accuracy, and adherence to reporting procedures. If any discrepancies are found that need to be corrected, feedback is provided to employees as appropriate detailing what needs to be revised or clarified. Additionally, supervisory officials in three of the five field divisions we spoke with reported that they maintain regular communication to help ensure that employees are completing investigations in an accurate and timely manner. DEA officials also reported that group supervisors work with Diversion Investigators on-site when necessary to help advise them on the appropriate steps to take during an investigation. Whenever a case is being elevated for disciplinary action (civil or criminal), Division management presents a summary of the case to the program manager detailing the facts and rationale for the disciplinary action. Division management reviews the case summary and determines approval for further action (e.g., prosecution).

In addition to direct supervisory review of work products, DEA's Office of Inspections also has a Self-Inspection Program (SIP) in which DEA field divisions are required to conduct annual self-inspections of five major program areas: enforcement management; enforcement effectiveness; financial management; confidential source management; and evidence.

According to the DEA officials we spoke with, during the on-site inspection process, field division group supervisors inspect each others' group case files to determine if investigations were conducted in accordance with required policies and procedures. Supervisory officials in all five field divisions we spoke with stated that they conduct the self-inspections on an annual basis. The results of the self-inspection reports are reviewed by the Office of Inspections. According to DEA's 2009-2014 Strategic Plan, information related to the SIP is used as the starting point for the Office of Inspection's cyclic, on-site inspections.

The Chief of the Diversion Control Program's Regulatory Section reported that field division officials submit to headquarters for review a copy of the investigative reports for every regulatory investigation that has been conducted.[23] DEA officials then conduct a quality review of these reports which assists them in identifying deficiencies and determine the training needs of diversion personnel as they relate to completing regulatory investigations. The chief of the Diversion Control Program's Regulatory Section stated that if report errors are identified during the review process, officials in the Regulatory Section follow up with the respective field division to address the issue and submit supplemental report information.

The Office of Inspections also conducts on-site internal inspections of DEA's 21 field divisions to ensure that employees are following required program policies and procedures—in accordance with the Diversion Investigator manual. The office's primary objective for on-site inspections of the diversion control program is to determine how the diversion control work is being conducted by the field divisions and identify and address any problems. According to the Chief Inspector the Office of Inspections, it is the Office of Inspection's goal to conduct on-site inspections every 3 years as resources allow. See figure 3 for a description of the steps involved in the internal inspection report process:

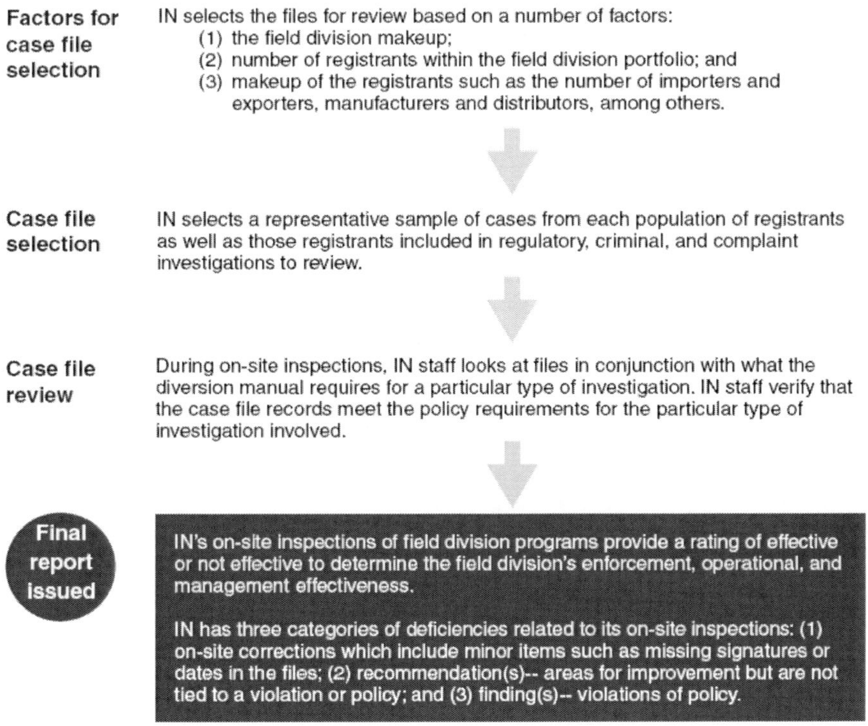

Source: DEA's Office of Inspections.

Figure 3. Description of On-Site Internal Inspection Process.

According to DEA officials, the Office of Inspections briefs headquarters-level management about the issues identified, and sends the report to the field division. For findings, the field division then has 60 days to provide a written response about the corrective actions that the field division has taken or plans to take. DEA officials also reported that they use internal inspections as an internal management tool to review their areas of responsibility. We reviewed DEA's most recent inspection reports available for each of its 21 field divisions which summarized the results of interviews with management and staff, reviews of program operations, and case files reviews for policy compliance, among other items.[24] We found that the inspections did not identify widespread findings or issues related to the timeliness and overall quality of the diversion investigations.

DEA Could Better Identify and Report on the Results of Its Diversion Control Efforts

Given DEA's increased focus on regulatory and criminal investigations in response to growing prescription drug diversion, it is critical for DEA to determine and report on the extent to which these additional efforts are helping to reduce diversion. In this regard, DEA has established performance measures to assess and report on its progress towards meeting its performance goal of reducing the diversion of licit drugs, but could enhance its set of performance measures to better capture and report on investigative outcomes and their results on diversion. We have previously reported that performance information can be used to help decide among competing priorities and allocate resources in a results-oriented management system.[25] Such performance information allows program managers to compare their programs' results with goals and thus help determine where to target resources to improve performance. In addition, one of the key characteristics of successful hierarchies of performance measures is the ability of the measures to demonstrate how well a program is achieving its goals.[26] As shown in table 2, DEA has developed five measures to track and publicly report the progress and results of its efforts in reducing the diversion of licit drugs.

According to DEA program officials, these measures were selected as a result of a performance measure review by the Department of Justice (DOJ) in 2009. For this review, DOJ asked all of its components to reexamine their performance measures to identify and discontinue performance measures that were confusing or did not adequately reflect the core mission. In place of such measures, DOJ asked the components to develop five core measures that are easy to understand and explain what is being accomplished with the resources expended. Our analysis of the measures found that while some indicate results, such as the number of organizations disrupted or dismantled that were involved in diverting prescription drugs, when taken together, the set of measures does not clearly demonstrate to what extent the additional efforts DEA has made in investigations in recent years are having an effect on the diversion problem.

Table 2. Performance Measures for DEA's Diversion Control Program

Milestones for development, implementation, and maintenance of the Rapid TargetingOnline Reports Tool (RapTOR)
Number of Diversion Priority Target Organizations (PTOs)[a] not linked to ConsolidatedPriority Organization Target (CPOT)[b] targets disrupted/dismantled[c]
Number of Diversion PTOs linked to CPOT targets disrupted/dismantled
Number of planned scheduled regulatory investigations completed
Number of Administrative/Civil/Criminal Sanctions

Source: DEA.

Notes:

[a] Priority Target Organizations are defined as drug trafficking organizations with an identified hierarchy engaged in the highest levels of drug trafficking and/or drug money laundering operations, having a significant international, national, regional, or local impact upon drug availability. According to DEA, the disruption or dismantlement of the organization will have a significant impact upon drug trafficking and/or money laundering activities and warrant the dedication of significant resources to achieve this end.

[b] Consolidated Priority Organization Targets (CPOTs) are defined as the command and control element of a major international drug trafficking organization and/or money laundering enterprise that significantly impacts the U.S. drug supply as identified by Organized Crime Drug Enforcement Task Forces member agencies. An organization is considered "linked" to a CPOT, if credible evidence exists of a nexus between the primary target of the investigation and a CPOT target. With the nature of the Diversion program, linkages to these international drug trafficking and money laundering organizations are a rare event.

[c] According to DEA, a disruption is defined as significantly impeding the normal and effective operation of a targeted organization, as indicated by changes in organizational leadership, trafficking patterns, drug production methods, etc. Examples of this may be seen in changes in price/purity of the drug or changes in methods of operation; increases in fees paid to couriers or transporters; movement of the organization to a neighboring district; and/or a reduction in availability of a drug on the streets, even if only temporarily. Dismantlement is defined as destroying the organization's leadership, financial base, and drug supply network such that the organization is incapable of operating and/or reconstituting itself.

As a result, the set of measures do not clearly explain how they demonstrate progress towards the overall program performance goal of reducing diversion. DEA program officials acknowledged that these measures do not fully reflect the results of the program towards the reduction of diversion and as a result, they do not rely on them exclusively for managing the program or determining where best to allocate program resources. They stated that for the purposes of internal program planning and management, they have access to and utilize other data and measures not reported, or can pull up additional information on investigative results that provide more detail on what the program is achieving towards the reduction of diversion.

Overall Outcome Measure Does Not Demonstrate Program Results

DEA has designated an overall outcome measure to track the results of the diversion control program as a whole; however, this measure does not demonstrate program results.[27] This measure—Milestones for Development, Implementation, and Maintenance of Data Warehouse to Monitor Closed Distribution System—tracks the development of an information warehouse system DEA is developing for use in diversion investigations. According to DEA officials, when completed, this warehouse—known as the Rapid Targeting Online Reports Tool (RapTOR)—will facilitate data and trends analysis as part of diversion investigations. DEA officials explained that RapTOR is intended to streamline the investigation process by providing a comprehensive data warehouse tool that is linked to other DEA databases such as ARCOS, the drug theft/loss reporting system, and a system that tracks the number of asset forfeitures, arrests, and other enforcement data.

While the RapTOR appears to hold promise as a useful tool in diversion investigations, tracking the milestones of its development as the outcome measure for the overall diversion program does not demonstrate results or capture outcomes from the program as a whole as it is only one project within the program. According to OMB guidance to agencies on preparing strategic plans and performance reports, outcome measures are to describe the intended result of carrying out a program and define an event or condition that is external to the program and is of direct importance to the intended beneficiaries or the public.[28] While tracking milestones for the RapTOR's deployment may be useful as project-specific outcome measures, due to their focused nature they do not provide information on results of the diversion control program as a whole. For instance, reporting on RapTOR's testing and deployment status does not provide program management or other decision makers such as Congress information to indicate the results of DEA's regulatory and criminal investigations are having towards the reduction of diversion of licit drugs, the program's performance goal. Development of an outcome measure that more directly demonstrates the external results of the overall program could provide better information to DEA program managers and other decision makers such as Congress about program successes which could also help determine how to most effectively use resources. According to DEA's fiscal year 2012 budget submission, the RapTOR will allow for the development of an outcome measure. When asked if they planned to develop an outcome measure to replace the RapTOR, DEA officials indicated that until RapTOR is fully developed and implemented, it would be too soon to tell when a replacement outcome measure would be necessary. Furthermore, DEA officials could not explain how they use the RapTOR measure to show overall program results or outcomes or how it will be used to develop a measure that reports such results or outcomes.

Performance Measures Tracking Investigations of Priority Targets Demonstrate Results

Two of DEA's performance measures track results DEA has achieved through criminal investigations of priority targets. In April 2001, DEA implemented the Priority Target Organization (PTO) program as a strategic initiative to identify, target, investigate, and disrupt or dismantle drug trafficking and/or money laundering organizations having a significant impact on drug availability within the United States. Although the Diversion Control Program was not officially part of the DEA's Priority Targeting Program prior to fiscal year 2010, with the creation of Tactical Diversion Squads in every domestic DEA field division, the Diversion Control Program has since begun focusing on the identification of PTOs and their eventual disruption and dismantlement.

DEA has two separate measures to track the number of PTOs disrupted and dismantled—one for those with identified links to Consolidated Priority Organization Targets (CPOTs) and another for those without links to CPOTs. As a participant in the PTO program, the Diversion Control Program is required to report on these performance measures. Whereas PTOs are organizations with an identified hierarchy engaged in drug trafficking or drug money laundering operations, CPOTs are the command and control elements of a major international drug trafficking organization and/or money laundering enterprise that significantly impacts the U.S. drug supply. An example of a diversion PTO cited by DEA officials was a practitioner who prescribed large quantities of controlled substance pharmaceuticals for nonmedical purposes to "patients" from at least five different states. DEA officials stated examples of CPOTs involved in diversion include international chemical distributors that traffic in chemicals used to manufacture methamphetamine while other CPOTs traffic in pharmaceuticals or counterfeit pharmaceuticals.

Specifically, these measures report the extent to which DEA disrupted (disrupt) or stopped (dismantle) the operations of PTOs and these organizations' ability to divert controlled substances, which helps to reduce the diversion of licit drugs, the program's overall performance goal.[29] For example in fiscal year 2010, DEA reported that it disrupted one PTO with linkages to a CPOT and dismantled one PTO with CP OT linkages. For PTOs without linkages to a CPOT, DEA reported disrupting 96 and dismantling 65 in fiscal year 2010. According to DEA officials, the PTO-related measures are useful in helping the program to focus criminal investigations on those priority targets against which they are likely to have the greatest impact on the diversion of licit drugs.

Other Performance Measures Do Not Clearly Demonstrate Results of Regulatory Investigations

While DEA has some performance measures to demonstrate the results of its criminal investigations, it lacks measures that clearly track resulting outcomes DEA has achieved through its additional regulatory investigations. For example, DEA has a measure that provides a numerical count of the scheduled or regulatory investigations completed. According to DEA's Fiscal Year 2009-2014 Strategic Plan, one of the objectives for the diversion control program is to ensure 98 percent compliance of all registrants by fiscal year 2014. However, while the performance measure is focused on the regulatory investigations and provides a count of the number of investigations completed, this measure does not demonstrate the results of those completed investigations or give a sense as to the extent to which registrants were found to comply with the CSA and thereby the extent to which DEA is achieving its stated objective. According to DEA officials, while they previously reported on the compliance rate of a subset of wholesale registrants as the program's outcome measure, the reexamination of program performance measures in 2009 resulted in discontinuing use of the measure. DEA officials stated that because the compliance level among registrants tends to be very high in general, the values of the measure did not significantly change from year to year. Consequently, they stated, the measure did not provide a meaningful gauge of the results regulatory investigations were having. However, DEA data reported before it discontinued use of this measure showed that the compliance rate, while always relatively high, fluctuated between 88.5 percent to as high as 97.7 percent between fiscal years 2003 and 2008. Further, as stated in DEA's strategic plan, one of the key objectives of the program is to ensure a certain level of compliance among registrants.[30] Without the reporting of a measure that directly tracks a level of compliance among registrants, the public and other external stakeholders such as Congress will not be able to determine the extent to which DEA is achieving that specific objective. In addition, given that DEA more than tripled the number of regulatory investigations conducted from fiscal year 2009 to fiscal year 2010 including investigations of previously excluded registrant groups as well as increasing the frequency of investigations for a rapidly growing DWP registrant group—it will be important for DEA to be able to assess and report on the potential results these additional investigations are having on regulatory compliance.

In addition, the other performance measure reports on the number of sanctions DEA has taken against diverters or noncompliant registrants over the past year. As such, it is one indicator of the results of DEA investigations. However, as it is a count of the sanctions, it only demonstrates the number of sanctions taken, but does not provide context as to the severity of the sanctions or the reason for the sanctions. For example, administrative sanctions resulting from deficiencies in a registrant's recordkeeping found during regulatory inspections may reflect a lack of compliance with the CSA but not necessarily instances of actual diversion. In contrast, criminal sanctions, such as prison time given to an individual or registrant for diversion of controlled substances, reflect sanctions taken against actual diversion that has occurred and identified during a criminal investigation. Because the sanctions are tallied together for the performance measure, it is difficult to determine to what extent they have resulted from regulatory noncompliance issues or instances of criminal diversion.

Another difficulty with combining the total number of administrative, civil, and criminal sanctions in one total is that changes in the number of the respective type of penalties mean different things in terms of what they indicate about the potential risk for diversion. For example, an increase in the number of criminal sanctions resulting from DEA's criminal investigations indicates that individuals or PTOs involved in diversion have been disrupted or dismantled, reducing the potential risk for future diversionary activities, and is therefore a desirable change. However, an increase in the number of administrative sanctions resulting from regulatory investigations could indicate a trend of rising noncompliance among registrants, which is an undesirable change as it implies that DEA's outreach efforts with industry may not have been effective and the potential risk for diversion is higher as a result of registrants' noncompliance. As a result, this measure does not provide a clear indication as to the effect DEA's investigative efforts are having on the problem of diversion. By tracking sanctions resulting from regulatory noncompliance combined with sanctions resulting from criminal diversion, program managers and other decision makers may lack information on what type of noncompliance is increasing and be able to determine what adjustments to the program's efforts, if any, might be necessary to address the root causes of increases in the number of sanctions.

DEA officials acknowledged that this measure by itself is not detailed enough to provide that information. However, they stated they supplement the measure for internal program planning and management functions by conducting analyses that separate out the different types of sanctions and provide more meaningful data on the sanctions to identify diversion trends, determine the results of their efforts, and inform future program plans and policy decisions. Officials also noted that providing a single count of sanctions without breaking them out helped simplify the measure and meet DOJ's goal of limiting the number of overall performance measures to five. While this may be more manageable for the purpose of providing performance information, the measure does not clearly tie to outcomes and demonstrate program performance—a key goal of DOJ's performance measure reexamination effort—and does not provide sufficiently meaningful information and data to external stakeholders and policy makers such as Congress about the types of sanctions DEA has taken as a result of both regulatory and criminal investigations.

Conclusions

The growing problem of controlled substance diversion presents a serious and constantly evolving threat to public health and safety. In responding to this threat, DEA faces a unique challenge in being proactive to investigate and stop the diversion of controlled prescription drugs and substances, while at the same time, ensure that individuals with legitimate needs and uses for such substances can obtain them. In recent years, DEA has taken steps to adjust its approach to increase its efforts in conducting regulatory and criminal investigations to facilitate registrant compliance with the CSA and enhance coordination and leverage the resources and abilities of other federal, state, and local partners when conducting investigations into criminal diversion. Given the steps DEA has taken, it is important for DEA management to track the results its efforts are having against diversion in order to determine what benefits are being realized and what, if any, adjustments need to be made to make them more effective.

DEA has established a set of performance measures for the program, but the link between most of the measures and how they demonstrate the progress DEA is making towards the overall goal of reducing diversion is unclear. Making more meaningful information available externally about the program's results would enable program managers and external stakeholders to better understand what the program is accomplishing and provide more effective oversight. By developing an outcome measure that demonstrates program wide results of benefit to the public and revising other performance measures to better track and report on the results of investigations and their results on reducing diversion of prescription drugs, DEA could make the measures more effective for demonstrating results. Doing so could also provide DEA program managers and other decision makers such as Congress better information to target program approaches accordingly to further optimize results against diversion.

RECOMMENDATION FOR EXECUTIVE ACTION

In order for DEA to better determine to what extent its efforts are decreasing diversions and to inform future program decisions, we recommend that the Administrator of DEA strengthen the agency's performance measurement for the Diversion Control Program by reassessing its set of performance measures for the program to identify ways to enhance the measures and their link to the program outcome goal of reducing diversion.

AGENCY COMMENTS AND OUR EVALUATION

We requested comments on a draft of this report from DOJ. DEA provided written comments, which are summarized below. In its comments, DEA stated it would take action to address the recommendation to strengthen its set of performance measures for the Diversion Control Program but that it disagreed with the finding that its performance measures do not adequately measure how its efforts reduce diversion or that such deficiencies impede resource allocation decisions. In an e-mail received on August 4, 2011, the Acting Assistant Director of DOJ's Audit Liaison Group clarified DEA's position stating that DEA did not concur with the recommendation.

In its comment letter and attachment, DEA stated that the report demonstrated that its management is appropriately directing its resources towards key points of diversion and confirms that DEA has been successful in accomplishing its objectives. DEA reiterated that performance measures must be viewed within the context of other information to assess the results that DEA efforts have on public health and safety as well as the reduction of diversion. To this end, DEA stated that its leadership provides policy makers and legislators information though a variety of other sources such as budget requests, intelligence reports, briefings, and testimonies. They also noted that the majority of such information presented to policy makers is based on investigative data and intelligence which is broader in scope than performance measures. In regards to developing or implementing measures to track regulatory performance, DEA stated that further strengthening the current performance measures to include regulatory performance measures would not provide any additional benefit in assisting the agency or other decision makers in the allocation of resources or targeting of program approaches to further optimize results. DEA stated that it would be extremely difficult to do so because the vast majority of registrant inspections do not uncover serious violations of the CSA and thus a very small number of registrants are subject to sanctions during the annual inspection cycle. Further, DEA stated that the deterrent effect of regulatory investigations cannot be quantified making it impossible to measure the lack of diversion resulting from DEA's efforts.

As the report indicates, we recognize that DEA has taken steps to allocate resources and position the program to respond to emerging diversion trends. However, the report does not state that DEA management has appropriately directed its resources or confirm that DEA has been successful in accomplishing its objectives. The review on which this report is based describes how DEA manages its investigations to address the growing and evolving nature of diversion and did not evaluate those actions for their efficiency or effectiveness as implied by DEA. At the same time, as our evidence did not suggest that DEA's use of current performance measures has directly impeded its resource allocation decisions to date, we made changes to the report to minimize any inference of such a finding. Moreover, the fact that a program may appear well managed on the basis of anecdotal and qualitative evidence does not negate the need or obligation for an agency to develop and use performance measures that hold it accountable for determining, articulating, and reporting what a program is accomplishing.

As performance measurement is a key part of an agency being results-oriented, that is, tracking and being held accountable for the results or outcomes an agency produces through its programs, our recommendation is intended to ensure that the program's performance measures meet the standards for performance measures established by DOJ and OMB and are the best measures possible to demonstrate and report the program's results to program management, other external decision makers such as Congress, as well as the public. We agree that program managers and decision makers can and should use other relevant program information in addition to performance measures when allocating resources and making program decisions. However, this also does not negate the need or obligation for an agency to develop and use performance measures that meet the standards established by DOJ and OMB. On the basis of our evaluation of the program's performance measures against the guidance and criteria for performance measures provided by DOJ and OMB, as well as our previous work on performance measurement, we believe that further refinements to the program's performance measures are merited and have the potential to help make the measures provide more useful information on the achievements of the program.

Because many outside parties, such as industry members and the American public, may not have access to other contextual information DEA may provide policy makers and legislators, refinement of the current set of program performance measures could enable DEA to better assess and externally report on the results of the program in a more meaningful and understandable way. As DOJ guidance to component agencies suggests, performance measures should clearly articulate what an agency is accomplishing with the resources used in language outsiders can understand. Some of the key measures DEA is using do not meet this standard. For example, according to DEA, tracking the milestones for the development, implementation, and maintenance of the program's Rapid Targeting Online Reports Tool (RapTOR) was chosen as the program's outcome measure so that managers could monitor the development and implementation of the system to ensure it was done in a timely and cost-efficient manner. While we agree that project schedule and cost should be closely monitored, this measure does not articulate to outsiders what the program is accomplishing as called for by DOJ's guidance for performance measures. Further, given that the RapTOR is an internal data warehouse tool DEA is developing, the reporting of milestones for the development, implementation, and maintenance of the tool does not provide an overall indicator of success for DEA's diversion program or its stated goal of reducing the diversion of licit drugs. As a result, it also does not meet OMB's criteria that requires outcome measures to describe or capture an event or condition external to the program that is of importance to the public. Indeed, DEA program officials could not describe how they use this measure more broadly beyond tracking the progress of the project itself.

In regards to developing or implementing a performance measure to track the impact of the regulatory inspection process, we disagree with DEA that including a regulatory performance measure would not provide any additional benefit. DEA stated that it would be extremely difficult to develop such a measure because the vast majority of registrant inspections do not uncover serious violations and thus sanctions are taken against a very small number of registrants. While this may be the case, reporting the number of administrative, civil, and criminal sanctions taken as a single count as DEA currently does, does not provide perspective as to how many sanctions are a result of regulatory infractions and how many are a result of criminal infractions. Also, as DEA points out, the severity of sanctions and their impacts can vary greatly ranging from requiring on-site corrections by a registrant for minor infractions to DEA pursuing legal sanctions against a registrant which could have a profound effect on the wider registrant population as a whole. Given the differences between regulatory sanctions and criminal sanctions and the potential severity of different sanction types, we continue to believe it would be useful for DEA to develop a measure that separately tracks the results of regulatory investigations or the number and severity of regulatory sanctions taken for identified infractions. With such a measurement, more information would be available to program managers, other decision makers, and the public on what type of noncompliance, if any, is increasing and thereby decision makers would be better able to determine what adjustments to the program's efforts, if any, might be necessary to address the causes of increases in the number of sanctions.

In terms of tracking the lack of diversion or similarly, the reduction in diversion resulting from DEA's efforts, DEA stated that it would be impossible to measure. However, given that one of the key program objectives DEA identified in its strategic plan is ensuring a level of compliance with the CSA among DEA registrants, whose compliance in turn directly maintains the closed system of distribution established by the CSA, it is important that DEA have a performance measure that directly links to this objective. We and OMB have acknowledged the difficulty in developing measures for programs that aim to deter or prevent specific behaviors, and have reported that in such instances proxy measures should be designed to assess the effectiveness of program functions. Proxy measures can be used to assess the effectiveness of program functions rather than directly assess the effectiveness of the program. In this regard, one possible approach DEA could use is to develop a proxy measure that tracks the compliance rate of wholesale registrants based on the results of regulatory investigations completed that year. Also, OMB has pointed out, it may be necessary to have a number of proxy measures to help ensure sufficient safeguards are in place to account for performance results.

Given the significant and growing problem of the diversion and abuse of pharmaceutical-controlled substances in the United States, having a set of performance measures that clearly conveys the accomplishments of the Diversion Control program is perhaps even more important now. By reassessing the program's current performance measures and making changes where necessary to the measures, DEA will be in a better position to provide enhanced information to program managers, other decision makers such as Congress, and the public on the extent to which the program is achieving its stated longer range performance goal of reducing diversion.

DEA also provided technical comments, which we incorporated as appropriate.

Eileen Regen Larence
Director,
Homeland Security and Justice Issues

End Notes

[1] Pub. L. No. 91-513, tit. II, 84 Stat. 1236, 1242-84 (codified as amended at 21 U.S.C. §§ 801-890, 901-971). According to the CSA, the term "controlled substance" means a drug or other substance, or immediate precursor, that is included in one of five classification schedules. A controlled substance is placed in a respective schedule based on whether it has a currently accepted medical use in treatment in the United States and its relative abuse potential and likelihood of causing dependence. The order of the schedules reflects substances that are progressively less dangerous and addictive. The term "controlled substance" as used in this report includes controlled prescription drugs.

[2] Substance Abuse and Mental Health Services Administration, Office of Applied Studies, *The TEDS Report: Substance Abuse Treatment Admissions Involving Abuse of Pain Relievers: 1998 and 2008*. (Rockville, Md.: July 15, 2010).

[3] Given the limitations and uncertainties of the methods and sources used in this study, these results should be interpreted with caution and regarded as approximations only. See Ryan N. Hansen, Gerry Oster, John Edelsberg, George E. Woody, and Sean D. Sullivan,

"Economic Costs of Nonmedical Use of Prescription Opiods," *Clinical Journal of Pain*, vol. 27, no. 3 (2011).

[4] We have previously issued reports related to the diversion and abuse of prescription drugs. See GAO, *Medicaid: Fraud and Abuse Related to Controlled Substances Identified in Selected States*, GAO-09-957 (Washington, D.C.: September 2009); GAO, *Prescription Drugs: OxyContin Abuse and Diversion and Efforts to Address the Problem*, GAO-04-110 (Washington, D.C.: December 2003); and GAO, *Prescription Drugs: State Monitoring Programs Provide Useful Tool to Reduce Diversion*, GAO-02-634 (Washington, D.C.: May 2002).

[5] We are currently conducting a separate review examining the trends in misuse and abuse of prescription pain relievers and how federal agencies, including DEA, educate the public and health care providers about misuse and abuse of such drugs.

[6] We reviewed DEA's budget justification submissions for fiscal years 2008 to 2012 because we wanted to review the five most recent budget justifications available.

[7] We reviewed DEA data on case volumes for investigations and data on the number of personnel working on DEA's Tactical Diversion Squads for fiscal years 2007 to 2010 because we wanted to focus our analysis on the most recent 4-year period. Tactical Diversion Squads are teams of DEA diversion personnel, as well as other federal, state, and local law enforcement personnel, whose mission is to detect, investigate, disrupt, and refer for prosecution, violators of federal and state controlled substance statutes pertaining to drug diversion.

[8] GAO, *Standards for Internal Control in the Federal Government*, GAO/AIMD 00-21.3.1 (Washington, D.C.: November 1999). Internal control is an integral component of an organization's management that provides reasonable assurance that the following objectives are being achieved: effectiveness and efficiency of operations, reliability of financial reporting, and compliance with applicable laws and regulations. These standards, issued pursuant to the requirements of the Federal Managers' Financial Integrity Act of 1982 (FMFIA), provide the overall framework for establishing and maintaining internal control in the federal government. Also pursuant to FMFIA, the Office of Management and Budget issued Circular A-123, revised December 21, 2004, to provide the specific requirements for assessing the reporting on internal controls. Internal control standards and the definition of internal control in Circular A-123 are based on GAO's *Standards for Internal Control in the Federal Government*.

[9] We reviewed the on-site internal inspection reports for DEA's 21 field divisions for fiscal years 2005 to 2010 because we requested DEA to provide the most recent internal inspection report available from each field division. The inspection reports DEA provided in response to this request varied in date from fiscal year 2005 to 2010.

[10] GAO, *Executive Guide: Effectively Implementing the Government Performance and Results Act*, GAO/GGD-96-118 (Washington, D.C.: June 1996); GAO, *Agencies Annual Performance Plans Under the Results Act: An Assessment Guide to Facilitate Congressional Decisionmaking* GAO/GGD/AIMD-10.1.18 (Washington, D.C.: February 1998); and GAO, *Tax Administration: IRS Needs to Further Refine Its Tax Filing Season Performance Measures*, GAO-03-143 (Washington, D.C.: November 2002).

[11] 21 U.S.C. § 812. The act also authorizes the Attorney General to promulgate regulations adding, moving, or removing a drug or substance to, among, or from the five schedules established by the act after making certain findings specified by statute.

[12] According to DEA officials, the locations for the additional squads were based on proximity to major cities, availability of office space within the DEA field divisions, the reported needs

of local areas for a task force focused on diversion investigations, and the interest and ability of state and local law enforcement agencies to provide task force officers.

[13] In October 1992, Congress passed the Departments of Commerce, Justice and State, the Judiciary and Related Agencies Appropriations Act of 1993 which changed the source of funding for DEA's Diversion Control Program from being part of DEA's congressional appropriation to full funding by registration and reregistration fees. The act required that the fees charged by DEA under its diversion control program be set at a level to recover the costs of operating the program.

[14] DEA registrants (practitioner, hospital/clinic, retail pharmacy, and teaching institution) that fall under the business activity category "Dispensing or Instructing" pay a registration fee once every 3 years.

[15] These participants volunteered this information. Because these officials volunteered this information, we do not know the extent to which other squad officials share this view.

[16] Pub. L. No. 106-310, tit. XXXV, 114 Stat. 1101, 1222-27 (2000).

[17] 21 U.S.C. § 823(g).

[18] These registrant types include manufacturers, bulk manufacturers, distributors, importers/exporters, and bulk importers.

[19] 21 C.F.R. § 1301.74(b).

[20] According to DEA officials, of the 60 Diversion Investigator positions requested for fiscal year 2011, as of May 2011, 34 positions have been allocated.

[21] DEA headquarters officials told us that they are in the process of revising the Diversion Investigator and Special Agent manuals to address new laws, regulations, and policies concerning the Diversion Control Program and that they anticipate completing revisions to the manuals by fall 2011.

[22] The Basic Diversion Investigator course is divided into five segments covering the following subject areas including: (1) an overview of diversion control, (2) techniques for diversion investigations, (3) the laws and regulations governing the Diversion Control Program, (4) an overview of chemical diversion control, and (5) criminal investigations. Within these segments, the training covers issues such as the policies and procedures for conducting different types of diversion investigations, documenting investigations, determining the appropriate sanctions to apply in cases of noncompliance, and processes for supervisory review of the work.

[23] DEA's Regulatory Section (ODG) has oversight of regulatory matters under the Diversion Control Program (DCP) such as administrative or civil action taken against a registrant pursuant to the CSA and promulgated regulations. ODG also monitors field regulatory investigative activities such as periodic scheduled cyclic investigations, preregistration investigations, Order to Show Cause investigations, and drug theft/loss investigations, among other investigations.

[24] The most recent reports available ranged in issue date from fiscal year 2005 to 2010.

[25] GAO/GGD-96-118; GAO, *Results-Oriented Government: Using GPRA to Address 21st Century Challenges,* GAO-03-1166T (Washington, D.C.: Sept. 18, 2003); GAO, *Results-Oriented Budget Practices in Federal Agencies,* GAO-01-1084SP (Washington, D.C.: August 2001); and GAO, *Human Capital: Key Principles for Effective Strategic Workforce Planning,* GAO-04-39 (Washington, D.C.: December 2003).

[26] As we discussed in our June 1996 guide on implementing the Government Performance and Results Act, we studied a number of leading public sector organizations that were pursuing management reform initiatives and becoming more results-oriented. As part of these initiatives we found leading organizations seek to establish clear hierarchies of performance

goals and measures, linking the goals and performance measures for each organizational level to successive levels and ultimately to the organization's strategic goals. Based on this study of leading public sector organizations, we found that at least four characteristics are common to successful hierarchies of performance measures: (1) Demonstrate results; (2) Limited to the vital few; (3) Respond to multiple priorities; and (4) Link to responsible programs. As our focus of this review was on how DEA determines the results of its efforts against the diversion problem, we limited our analysis of DEA's performance measures to the characteristic of "Demonstrate results."

[27] Performance measures may address the type or level of program activities conducted (process), the direct products and services delivered by a program (outputs), or the results of those products and services (outcomes). See GAO-11-646SP.

[28] OMB Circular A-11 PART 6 Section 200.4, July 2010.

[29] Under disruptions, registrants usually retain the DEA Registration with restrictions and/or financial penalty. Registrants may also be temporarily denied access to controlled substances/chemicals. Under dismantlements, registrants lose or forfeit their DEA Registration or are convicted of a drug felony. Registrants are permanently denied access to controlled substances/chemicals pending a reversal of circumstances.

[30] DEA's Fiscal Year 2009-2014 Strategic Plan states that a 6-year objective for the program is to "ensure CSA compliance among 98 percent of all registrants by the end of fiscal year 2014."

In: Prescription Drugs
Editors: J. J. Phillips and W. O. Penny ISBN 978-1-62081-211-2

Chapter 3

STATEMENT OF MICHELE M. LEONHART, ADMINISTRATOR, DRUG ENFORCEMENT ADMINISTRATION. HEARING ON "RESPONDING TO THE PRESCRIPTION DRUG EPIDEMIC: STRATEGIES FOR REDUCING ABUSE, MISUSE, DIVERSION, AND FRAUD"*

Chairman Whitehouse, Ranking Member Kyl, and distinguished Members of the Subcommittee, on behalf of the men and women of the Drug Enforcement Administration (DEA), I am honored to have the opportunity to appear before you today to provide testimony concerning the dangers of prescription drug abuse.

OVERVIEW

The diversion and abuse of pharmaceutical controlled substances is a significant and growing problem in the United States. Leading indicators show substantially high levels in the abuse and misuse (non-medical use) of these

* This is an edited, reformatted and augmented version of testimony given on May 24, 2011, before the Subcommittee on Crime and Terrorism, Committee on the Judiciary, United States Senate.

drugs and the consequences associated with such actions. These indicators include, but are not limited to: the National Survey on Drug Use and Health, Monitoring the Future Study, Partnership Attitude Tracking Study (PATS), Drug Abuse Warning Network (DAWN) data, Treatment Episode Data Set, American Poison Control Centers data, and the National Forensic Laboratory Information System (NFLIS).

- According to the Substance Abuse and Mental Health Services Administration's (SAMHSA's) 2009 National Survey on Drug Use and Health (NSDUH), 7 million Americans were current non-medical users of psychotherapeutic drugs, significantly higher by 12 percent compared to 2008. Over three-quarters of that number, 5.3 million Americans, abused pain relievers.
- The NSDUH survey also indicated that the non-medical use of prescription drugs was second only to marijuana abuse.
- On average, more than 7,000 people 12 years and older initiate use of a controlled substance pharmaceutical drug for non-medical purposes every day.
- The Centers for Disease Control and Prevention (CDC) reported that the number of poisoning deaths involving any opioid analgesics increased from 4,041 in 1999 to 14,459 in 2007, more than tripling in 8 years.[1]
- SAMHSA's Treatment Episode Data Set shows that between 1998 and 2008 the number of persons admitted for treatment that reported any pain reliever abuse increased more than fourfold.
- According to DAWN data, the number of emergency department visits involving the misuse or abuse of pharmaceuticals increased by 98.4 percent between 2004 and 2009. The prescription drugs most implicated were opiate/opioid pain relievers, oxycodone products increased 242 percent, and hydrocodone products increased 124 percent.
- The approximate number of cases submitted by state and local law enforcement to forensic labs between 2001 and 2009 increased significantly (330 percent for oxycodone, 314 percent for hydrocodone, and 281 percent for methadone).

Statistics concerning the abuse of pharmaceutical controlled substances and prescription medication also reveal disturbing trends. Persons aged 12 years and older who used prescription drugs non-medically in the past month exceeded the number of current users of cocaine, heroin, hallucinogens, and methamphetamine combined.[2] In this age range, prescription drug abuse is second only to marijuana use.[3] Another factor that may contribute to the overall upward trend of abuse is that teenagers and young adults believe that prescription medications are safer than other drugs of abuse such as heroin, cocaine, marijuana and methamphetamine. The 2008 PATS study noted that 41 percent of teenagers mistakenly believe that prescription medications are "much safer" than illegal drugs.[4] Because prescription medications are manufactured by pharmaceutical companies, prescribed by physicians and other medical professionals, and dispensed by pharmacists, teens and young adults often have a false sense of security regarding these potent and sometimes dangerous medications. This false sense of security can end in tragedy. In 2010, about 1 in 4 teens admitted to using a prescription drug not prescribed to them by a doctor at some point in their lives.[5] Teens continue to report that their parents do not talk to them about the risks of prescription drugs in the same manner as they discuss other substances of abuse.[6] The 2010 Monitoring the Future study reported that Vicodin, a brand name pain reliever containing the narcotic hydrocodone, is one of the most commonly abused drugs among 12th graders: in 2010, about 1 in 13 (8%) reported non-medical use in the previous year.[7] On average, every day 2,100 12-17 year olds abuse a prescription pain reliever for the first time.[8] The economic impact on the United States from the non-medical use of prescription opioids in 2006 was estimated at $53.4 billion, ($42 billion in lost productivity, $8.2 billion in criminal justice costs, $2.2 billion in treatment costs, and $944 million in medical complications).[9]

DRUG ENFORCEMENT ADMINISTRATION AND THE DIVERSION CONTROL PROGRAM

Under the Controlled Substances Act (CSA), Congress established a "closed system" of distribution designed to prevent the diversion of controlled substances. In furtherance of the closed system, no controlled substance may be transferred between two entities unless the entities are DEA registrants or exempt from registration.

To maintain the closed system, every entity that manufactures or distributes controlled substances, or proposes to engage in the manufacture or distribution of any controlled substance, must obtain a DEA registration authorizing such activity.

In addition to the requirement that DEA registrants maintain copious records of all transactions involving controlled substances, the closed system is monitored by the Automation of Reports and Consolidated Orders System (ARCOS).

The Automation of Reports and Consolidated Orders System (ARCOS)

The Automation of Reports and Consolidated Orders System (ARCOS) is DEA's database that captures controlled substance activity from the point of manufacture and/or distribution to the point of sale to the retail level registrant (e.g., pharmacies, hospitals, practitioners, teaching institutions, researchers, analytical labs, importers/exporters, and Narcotic Treatment Programs).

Approximately 1,100 manufacturers and distributors report data to ARCOS. Just under 70.9 million transactions were reported to ARCOS in 2010. Manufacturers of bulk and/or dosage form controlled substances must report inventories, acquisitions, and dispositions of all substances in schedules I and II, schedule III narcotics, and GammaHydroxybutyric Acid (GHB) in Schedule III.

Additionally, manufacturers must report synthesizing activities involving all substances in schedules I and II, schedule III narcotics, Gamma-Hydroxybutyric Acid (GHB) substances in schedule III, and selected psychotropic controlled substances in schedules III and IV.

Distributors of bulk and/or dosage form controlled substances must report inventories, acquisitions, and dispositions of all substances in schedules I and II, schedule III narcotics, and Gamma-Hydroxybutyric Acid (GHB) substances in schedule III.

Once the substance has been sold to the retail level registrant, ARCOS does not capture further transaction information (i.e., from practitioner to end user, from pharmacy to end user, etc.).

The Quota System

DEA establishes manufacturing and procurement quotas each year for schedule I and II controlled substances in order to avoid the overproduction of these substances, for the purpose of reducing the risk of diversion to illicit traffic. Accordingly, the quota system serves the vital purpose of reducing the risk of diversion. Pursuant to 21 U.S.C. § 826(a), the Attorney General is required to determine "the total quantity and establish production quotas for each basic class of controlled substance in schedule I and II . . . to be manufactured each calendar year to provide for the estimated medical, scientific, research, and industrial needs of the United States, for lawful export requirements, and for the establishment and maintenance of reserve stocks." These determinations, which are known as aggregate production quotas, "represent those quantities of controlled substances that may be produced in the United States in" the relevant calendar year. The aggregate production quota is then allocated among those registered manufacturers who apply for, and demonstrate a need for, a manufacturing quota.

Pursuant to DEA regulation, a registrant seeking a manufacturing quota is required to submit an application form justifying the quantity it seeks to manufacture. The completed form must provide, for the particular basic class, the data for the current and preceding 2 calendar years to include: 1) its authorized individual manufacturing quota; 2) the actual or estimated quantity manufactured; 3) the actual or estimated or net disposal; 4) the actual or estimated inventory allowance; and 5) the actual or estimated inventory as of December 31. In addition to the desired individual manufacturing quota which is being sought, the applicant is required to state any additional factors which the applicant finds relevant to the fixing of his individual manufacturing quota, including the trend of (and recent changes in) his and the national rate of net disposal, his production cycle and current inventory position, the economic and physical availability of raw materials for use in manufacturing and for inventory purposes, yield and stability problems, potential disruptions to production (including possible labor strikes) and recent unforeseen emergencies such as floods and fires.

Restructuring

The substantial increase in the abuse of prescription drugs is fueled by many factors, including the development and marketing of new controlled substances, and ever-changing methods of diversion such as rogue Internet pharmacy schemes or rogue pain clinics. Attempts to prevent, detect, and reduce the diversion and abuse of controlled substance pharmaceuticals continue to evolve. The DEA has taken action on several fronts over the past few years to help reduce this growing problem.

In October 2008, the then Acting Administrator authorized a two-pronged reorganization of the Diversion Control Program. The first prong involved a substantial expansion in the number of Tactical Diversion Squads (TDS) and their deployment throughout the United States. This approach would provide a significant increase in the number of Special Agents and Task Force Officers who possess the requisite law enforcement authorities needed when conducting criminal investigations, i.e. the ability to conduct surveillance, make arrests and execute search warrants. The second prong of the reorganization plan called for a renewed focus on DEA's regulatory oversight of more than 1.3 million DEA registrants.

Expansion of Tactical Diversion Squads

Tactical Diversion Squads (TDS) investigate suspected violations of the Controlled Substances Act and other appropriate Federal and state statutes pertaining to the diversion of controlled substance pharmaceuticals and listed chemicals. These unique groups combine the skill sets of Special Agents, Diversion Investigators, and Task Force Officers (who come from a variety of state and local law enforcement agencies). TDS groups are dedicated solely towards investigating, disrupting, and dismantling those individuals or organizations involved in diversion schemes (e.g., "doctor shopping," prescription forgery rings, and doctors or pharmacists who illegally divert controlled substance pharmaceuticals and listed chemicals). Tactical Diversion Squads develop sources of information and disseminate intelligence to appropriate elements for the development of leads and targets. As of May 13, 2011, DEA has 37 operational TDS groups. DEA plans to add 26 more TDS groups over the next few years. With the expansion of Tactical Diversion Squads across the U.S., the number of diversion-related criminal cases has increased. These Tactical Diversion Squads have also been able to increase the number of diversion-related Priority Target Organization (PTO) investigations. PTO investigations focus on those criminal organizations or groups that significantly impact local, regional or national areas of the country. In addition, the Special Agent (SA) and Task Force Officer (TFO) work hours dedicated to diversion-related criminal cases has also increased dramatically.

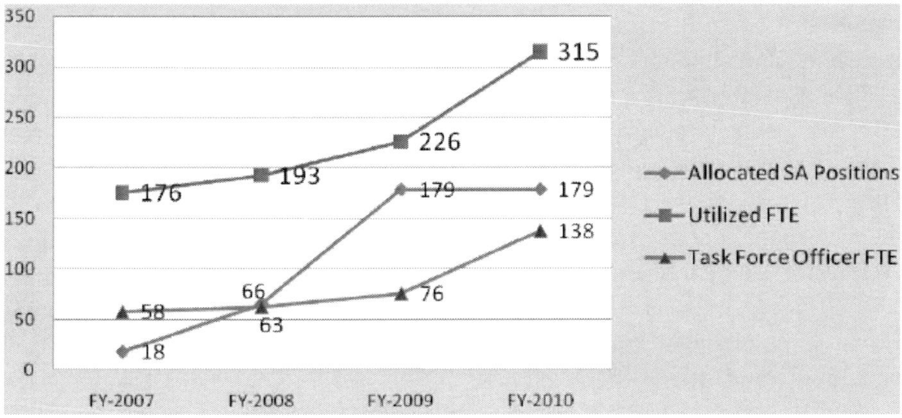

Figure 1. Special Agent and Task Force Officer FTE Utilization Diversion Control Program. FY-2007-FY2010.

Changes in Regulatory Investigations

As stated above, the second prong to the reorganization plan was to provide for enhanced regulatory oversight of more than 1.3 million registrants, a number which grows at an annual rate of approximately 2.5 percent. These registrants conduct a variety of business activities and vary in size and complexity. This portion of the plan required DEA to hire additional Diversion Investigators (DI) and create a new training curriculum. In FY 2009, the Office of Diversion Control developed and instituted this new training curriculum, which was designed to retrain and retool all Diversion Investigators in regulatory investigations. As of December 2010, all Diversion Investigators completed this training.

With more Diversion Investigators focused on the regulatory aspects of the Diversion Control Program, DEA increased the frequency of scheduled inspections to improve its regulatory oversight. As a result, the President's FY 2011 budget request of 60 more DI positions was authorized, and the FY 2012 budget requests an additional 50 DI positions. This renewed focus on regulatory control has enabled DEA to take a more proactive approach on multiple fronts to ensure that DEA registrants are complying with the Controlled Substances Act and implementing regulations. For example, DEA has revised its timetable regarding the frequency with which it will inspect/audit specific registrant categories such as controlled substance manufacturers (which includes bulk manufacturers); distributors; importers;

exporters; narcotic treatment programs; DATA-waived practitioners; researchers; and chemical handlers.

DEA's efforts are also aimed at ensuring that DEA registrants maintain effective controls against diversion by designing and operating systems that disclose to the registrant suspicious orders for controlled substances. In 2005, DEA established the Distributor Initiative Program to remind distributors of their responsibilities under the CSA and its implementing regulations concerning suspicious orders. Since its inception in August 2005 through May 13, 2011, DEA has briefed 75 DEA-registered corporations/companies comprising 215 distribution centers concerning illegal Internet pharmacy operations and rogue pain clinics. As a result, some distributors have voluntarily stopped selling or voluntarily restricted sales of controlled substances to certain domestic pharmacies and practitioners. Some distributors have also cut off the supply of controlled substance pharmaceuticals to certain customers as a result of their own intensified efforts spurred by the Distributor Initiative Program. From June 2006 through May 13, 2011, distributors have refused to sell controlled substances to approximately 1,517 customers that the distributors believed were placing suspicious orders for controlled substances.

DEA's enhanced regulatory oversight and investigative efforts have resulted in the identification of various distributors who failed to adhere to their regulatory responsibilities. Consequently, DEA took administrative action against these distributors, and also referred them for civil penalty action which resulted in record-breaking civil penalties negotiated with the registrant, e.g., $13.25 million civil penalty paid by McKesson Drug Corporation in April 2008; $34 million civil penalty paid by Cardinal Health in October 2008; and $75 million civil penalty in addition to $2.6 million in civil forfeitures against CVS Corporation in October 2010. And in April 2011, the Harvard Drug Group agreed to pay a civil penalty of $8 million.

Addition of Intelligence Research Specialist Positions

Due to the ever-increasing complexities of diversion investigations, another much-needed enhancement to the Diversion Control Program was the addition of Intelligence Research Specialists dedicated to working these types of investigations. Before FY 2006, the Diversion Control Program had no authorized Intelligence Research Specialist (IRS) positions allocated to the Program. In FY 2006, 40 IRS positions were allocated to the DCP with another 33 allocated in FY 2007. Even with this increase in positions, more

IRS work hours are attributed to the Diversion Control Program than are allocated. As a result, DEA requested and was authorized to increase by 14 IRS positions in the Diversion Control Program in FY 2011. In addition, another increase of 9 IRS positions is requested in FY 2012. The inclusion of this job series into the Diversion Control Program will help DEA conduct its investigations more efficiently and effectively.

Level of Effort by Drug Type

The restructuring of the Diversion Control Program has allowed investigative efforts to focus on specific problem areas, as shown in the charts below. For example, cases focused on oxycodone increased by 210 percent between FY 2005 and FY 2010, but have decreased for those involving hydrocodone, due to a significant decrease in domestic rogue internet pharmacies.

Between fiscal years 2006 and 2009, rogue Internet pharmacies were a major source of diversion. The rogue Internet pharmacies were responsible for the diversion of tens of millions of dosage units of hydrocodone. DEA responded to these rogue operations with investigations such as *Operation Baywatch, Operation CyberRx, Operation Lightning Strike, Operation TexRx, and Operation Control/Alt/Delete*. Although many domestic rogue Internet pharmacies that distributed controlled substances were eliminated after the Ryan Haight Act was implemented in April 2009, the problem has not been resolved with regard to foreign-based Internet pharmacies, and we continue to take steps to address it. In addition, rogue domestic Internet pharmacies selling mostly non-controlled substance and exempted[10] prescription drugs, including Carisoprodol, Tramadol, and what are commonly known as "lifestyle drugs," continue to pose a significant challenge.

What followed in the wake of these rogue Internet pharmacies was an almost immediate shift in the method of diversion and the type of pharmaceutical drugs being diverted. Today, a plethora of rogue pain clinics line the streets of south Florida. They supply drug seekers and pill distributors from up and down the entire East Coast with dangerous and powerful pharmaceuticals. Within these pill mills, the legitimate practice of medicine has given way to unadulterated greed. However, unlike the rogue Internet pharmacies, the practitioners at these rogue clinics are not dispensing hydrocodone, a schedule III controlled substance. They are dispensing and prescribing oxycodone, a schedule II controlled substance.

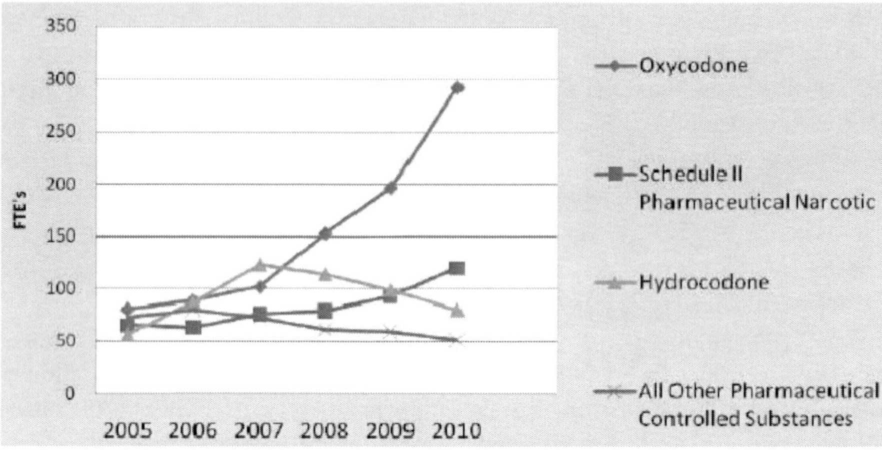

Figure 2. Diversion Control Program Core Personnel FTE Utilization by Top Four Drug Types FY-2005-FY2010.

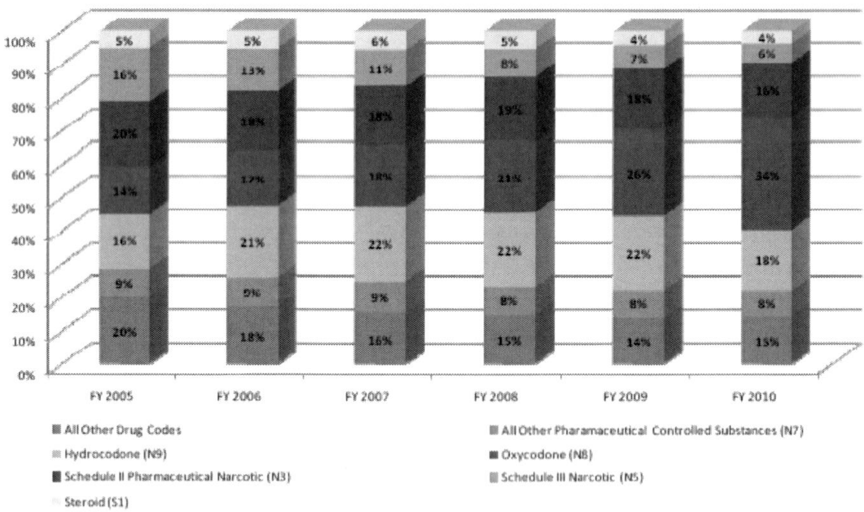

Figure 3. Percent of Diversion Cases Worked by Drug Type FY 2005- FY 2010.

This operation involved the mobilization of eleven Tactical Diversion Squads from across the United States to marshal with the Miami TDS and other state and local agencies in a concerted effort to attack and dismantle the hundreds of rogue pain clinics that continue to plague south Florida. On February 23, 2011, as part of *Operation Pill Nation* DEA conducted a coordinated effort with more than 500 state and local law enforcement officers in a massive takedown which included:

- 21 search warrants executed at clinics, residences, and other locations in south Florida;
- 25 arrested on various federal and state drug and money laundering charges, of which 5 were medical doctors and 5 were pain clinic owners;
- Seizure of approximately $7 million in assets ($3 million dollars in US currency and a variety of other real property, jewelry, and assets including 62 vehicles, some of which were exotic cars); and
- Immediate Suspension Orders issued against 14 DEA registrations, 1 Order to Show Cause issued against 3 DEA registrations, and the surrender of 7 DEA registrations.

As of April 12, 2011, *Operation Pill Nation* has resulted in the surrender of 83 DEA registrations (71 physicians, 8 pharmacies and 4 wholesale distributors); Immediate Suspension Orders issued against 63 DEA registrations (held by 37 physicians, 1 distributor); Orders to Show Cause issued against 6 DEA registrations; 38 clinics closed; and 32 arrests (12 physicians, 5 clinic owners and 15 clinic employees). Additionally, more than $16.4 million in assets have been seized thus far as a result of this operation ($11.9 million in US currency and approximately $4.5 million in vehicles, jewelry, real property, and other assets). One of the wholesale distributors has agreed to pay a civil fine of $8 million.

One component of the strategy for *Operation Pill Nation* is to identify the wholesale distributors that are supplying the controlled substances to these rogue pain clinics. In June 2010, DEA took administrative action against four wholesale distributors that were supplying rogue pain clinics in south Florida. Subsequent to that action, sales of oxycodone to dispensing practitioners in Florida plummeted. Florida also implemented legislation (effective October 2010) that limits a practitioner's ability to dispense controlled substance medications to what a patient would need in a 72-hour period.

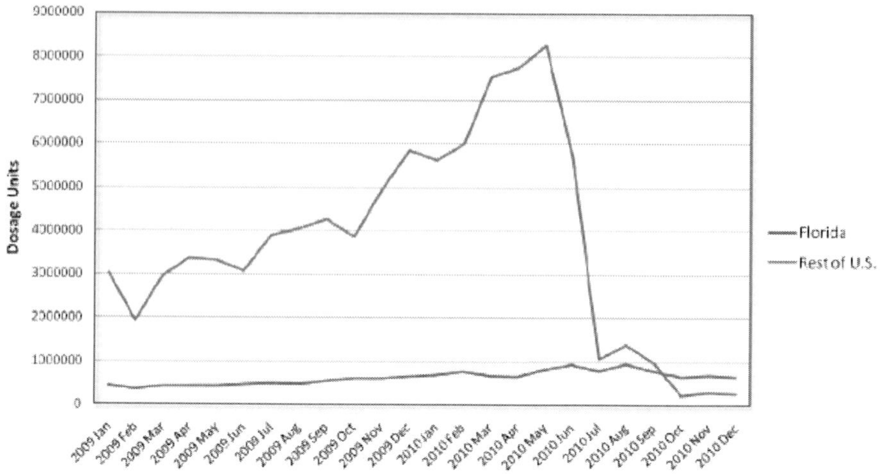

Figure 4. Monthly Oxycodone Sales to Practitioners, 2009-2010.

In addition to *Operation Pill Nation*, Tactical Diversion Squads and Diversion Groups across the United States continue to investigate large-scale diversion schemes. These investigations often result in the immediate suspension, revocation, or surrender of a registrant's DEA registration and in many cases in parallel civil and criminal proceedings.

THE FAMILY MEDICINE CABINET & PROPER DISPOSAL

Another factor that contributes to the increase of prescription drug abuse is the availability of these drugs in the household. In many cases, dispensed controlled substances remain in household medicine cabinets well after medication therapy has been completed, thus providing easy access to non-medical users for abuse, accidental ingestion, or illegal distribution for profit. Accidental ingestion of medication, including a controlled substance, by the elderly and children, is more likely when the household medicine cabinet contains unused medications that are no longer needed for therapy. The medicine cabinet also provides ready access to persons, especially teenagers, who seek to abuse medications. For example, the 2009 NSDUH indicates that 70 percent of Americans 12 and older who used pain relievers non-medically in the past year obtained the drugs from a friend or relative.[11] The Administration recognizes the issue of prescription drug abuse as described in the *National*

Drug Control Strategy. One of the action items set forth in the Strategy is to increase prescription return/take-back and disposal programs.[12]

On September 25, 2010, DEA coordinated the first-ever National Take-Back Initiative. Working with more than 3,000 state and local law enforcement partners, take-back sites were established at more than 4,000 locations across the United States. This massive undertaking resulted in the collection of 121 tons of unwanted or expired medications that were summarily disposed of.

In October 2010, Congress passed and the President signed into law the Secure and Responsible Drug Disposal Act of 2010. DEA has been working diligently to promulgate the regulations pertinent to this Act. On January 19 and 20, 2011, DEA conducted a public meeting to discuss the development of procedures for the surrender of unwanted controlled substances by ultimate users and long term care facilities. Specifically, this meeting allowed all interested persons—the general public including ultimate users, pharmacies, law enforcement personnel, reverse distributors, and other third parties—to express their views regarding safe and effective methods of disposal of controlled substances. The Act and implementing regulations will provide the basic framework that will allow Americans to dispose of their unwanted or expired controlled substance medications in a secure and responsible manner.

DEA is working diligently to promulgate disposal regulations. In the interim, DEA launched a second National Take-Back Initiative on April 30, 2011. Americans participating in the DEA's second nationwide event turned in more than 376,593 pounds (188 tons) of unwanted or expired medications for safe and proper disposal at the 5,361 take-back sites that were available in all 50 states, plus Guam, Puerto Rico, and in the U.S. Virgin Islands. This is 55 percent more than the 242,000 pounds (121 tons) the public brought in during last September's event.

The DEA's Take-Back events are a significant piece of the White House's prescription drug abuse prevention strategy released last month by the White House Office of National Drug Control Policy (ONDCP). Purging America's home medicine cabinets of neglected drugs is one of four action areas, or pillars, for reducing prescription drug abuse and diversion laid out in *Epidemic: Responding to America's Prescription Drug Abuse Crisis*. The other pillars include education of health care providers, patients, parents and youth; establishing prescription drug monitoring programs in all the states; and increased enforcement to address doctor shopping and pill mills.

Numerous national organizations joined the DEA and its state and local partners in putting on last April's Take Back Day, including ONDCP; the American Association of Poison Control Centers; the Community Anti-Drug

Coalitions of America; D.A.R.E. America; the Federation of State Medical Boards; various agencies of the U. S. Department of Health and Human Services; the International Association of Chiefs of Police; the National Association of Attorneys General; the National Family Partnership; the National Organization of Black Law Enforcement Executives; the National Association of Boards of Pharmacy; the National District Attorneys Association; the National Sheriffs' Association; and The Partnership at Drugfree.org.

CONCLUSION

Prescription drug abuse is a serious problem. DEA has the statutory responsibility of enforcing the Controlled Substances Act and its implementing regulations. Efforts towards this end help to minimize the availability of pharmaceutical controlled substances to non-medical users and preserve the integrity of the closed-system of distribution. Reducing prescription drug abuse is vital to the health and welfare of the American people and is a priority for this Administration.

Chairman Whitehouse, Ranking Member Kyl, and distinguished Members of the Subcommittee, thank you for the opportunity to appear today to discuss this important issue.

End Notes

[1] Centers for Disease Control and Prevention, Morbidity and Mortality Weekly Report, August 20, 2010.

[2] Substance Abuse and Mental Health Services Administration. Results from the 2009 National Survey on Drug Use and Health.

[3] Ibid, p. 14.

[4] Partnership for a Drug-Free America, 2008 Partnership Attitude Tracking Study, Key Findings.

[5] Partnership for a Drug-Free America, 2010 Partnership Attitude Tracking Study.

[6] 2010 Partnership Attitude Tracking Study, p.18.

[7] 2010 Monitoring the Future Study. University of Michigan, Ann Arbor.

[8] Substance Abuse and Mental Health Services Administration, 2009 National Survey on Drug Use and Health..

[9] Hansen, RN et al. 2011. "Economic costs of non-medical use of prescription opioids. *Clinical Journal of Pain*, Mar-April; 27(3):194-2-2.

[10] "Exempted prescription products" are prescription drugs that contain certain nonnarcotic controlled substances yet are exempt from some provisions of the Controlled Substances Act. 21 C.F.R. § 1308.32. One example of an exempted prescription product is butalbital

(brand name Fioricet), which would otherwise be a schedule III controlled substance because it contains a derivative of barbituric acid.

[11] Substance Abuse and Mental Health Services Administration. Results from the 2009 National Survey on Drug Use and Health.

[12] 2010 National Drug Control Strategy, p. 32

In: Prescription Drugs
Editors: J. J. Phillips and W. O. Penny
ISBN 978-1-62081-211-2

Chapter 4

STATEMENT OF JOHN L. EADIE, MPA, DIRECTOR, PRESCRIPTION MONITORING PROGRAM CENTER OF EXCELLENCE, BRANDEIS UNIVERSITY. HEARING ON "ENHANCING PRESCRIPTION MONITORING PROGRAMS ABILITY TO IMPEDE THE PRESCRIPTION DRUG ABUSE EPIDEMIC"*

Good morning Chairman Whitehouse and distinguished members of the Subcommittee. My name is John Eadie. I am the Director of the Prescription Monitoring Program Center of Excellence at Brandeis University. Thank you for the opportunity to appear before you on behalf of the Center to discuss our work on enhancing Prescription Monitoring Programs' ability to impede the prescription drug abuse epidemic. We thank you for the honor of testifying on this critical matter.

The PMP Center of Excellence seeks to help end the prescription drug abuse epidemic in the United States without compromising accepted standards of pain management or the legitimate prescribing of controlled substances. In collaboration with the Alliance of States with Prescription Monitoring Programs, the Center provides academically sound and practice-relevant informa-

* This is an edited, reformatted and augmented version of testimony given on May 24, 2011, before the Committee on the Judiciary, Subcommittee on Crime and Terrorism, United States Senate.

tion, evaluation, and expertise to PMPs and their stakeholders. The Center is funded by a grant from the Department of Justice Bureau of Justice Assistance.

Our work is focused on helping PMPs identify and implement the most effective means possible for them to intervene in the prescription drug abuse epidemic. Our work includes:

- Identifying PMP Best Practices, including innovative, cutting edge developments that will increase PMP effectiveness.
- Encouraging innovative uses of PMP data.
- Assisting in the deployment and evaluation of interstate PMP data sharing.
- Advancing the methodology for assessing PMP effectiveness to identify, improve and extend the applications of PMPs.
- Analyzing PMP performance measures and identifying improvements in measurement.
- Analyzing and disseminating relevant information through a clearinghouse.
- Providing support to states and federal agencies.

The urgency of our work is based upon our knowledge that:

- Daily, 50 people in our nation die from unintentional prescription opioid overdoses and
- Daily, twenty times that number are admitted to hospital emergency departments for opioid overdoses.

At the PMP Center of Excellence, we believe that we must improve our methods for identifying and interdicting prescription opioid abuse in order to slow down and reverse this epidemic's ever rising toll.

Prescription Monitoring Programs collect from pharmacies information regarding prescriber, pharmacy, patient, and drug information regarding each controlled substance prescription dispensed within their states and, in some cases, prescriptions sent by mail order into their states. The data is compiled in each PMP's database and then made available to prescribers, pharmacies, law enforcement, health professional licensing agencies, and, depending on the state, to Medicaid Programs, medical examiners, drug courts, drug treatment programs and others. De-identified data is generally made available to researchers and evaluators and patients may see their own data in some states.

The rapid growth in states with prescription monitoring programs, with 48 states now having statutorily authorized PMPs, is a very hopeful accomplishment. The majority of these programs have been authorized since 2003, when the Harold Rogers Prescription Drug Monitoring Programs Grant program began. Administered by the Department of Justice's Bureau of Justice Assistance, the Harold Rogers' competitive grant program has stimulated growth and enhancements among the PMPs.

Funding provided by the NASPER program, as administered by the Substance Abuse and Mental Health Administration, is a formula grant program that has been important in assisting states' PMPs by supporting their operations.

The continued operation of PMPs and the significant enhancements called for to address the prescription drug abuse epidemic appear to call for continuation and expansion of both unique programs.

In addition to federal funding support, we need a rapid evolution of the PMPs into a new generation of even more effective systems, a new generation whose hallmark must be proactivity. The new generation will take advantage of technological advances and integrate them into the fabric of PMP operations. Many of the characteristics of the new generation are highlighted in the White House Office of National Drug Control Policy's new Prescription Drug Abuse Prevention Plan.

INTERSTATE PMP DATA SHARING

The first thing that must be completed is a new National Network of State PMPs that are interoperable through the Prescription Monitoring Information Exchange (PMIX) Hub which BJA, the IJSI Institute, and the Alliance of States with Prescription Monitoring Programs have been working to establish for six years. The Hub is operational and several states are in process of interconnecting, with support from the PMP Training and Technical Assistance Program and our Center at Brandeis University.

PMP MODEL ACT PROVISIONS

The foundation for much of the new generation of PMPs rests in the Alliance of States with Prescription Monitoring Programs' *PRESCRIP-*

TION MONITORING PROGRAM MODEL ACT 2010 Revision at (www.pmpalliance.org).

Section 7, Providing Prescription Monitoring Information

(a) The [designated state agency or entity] should review the prescription information.

Such reviews should include but not be limited to:

I. A review to identify information that appears to indicate if a person may be obtaining prescriptions in a manner that may represent misuse or abuse of controlled substances. When such information is identified, the [designated state agency] should notify the practitioners and dispensers who prescribed or dispensed the prescriptions.

II. A review to identify information that appears to indicate if a violation of law or breach of professional standards may have occurred. Whenever such information is identified, the [designated state agency] should notify the appropriate law enforcement and/or professional licensing, certification or regulatory agency or entity, and provide prescription information necessary for an investigation.

(b) The [designated state agency] is authorized to provide information in the prescription monitoring program upon request only to the following persons.

I. Persons authorized to prescribe or dispense controlled substances or other drug required to be submitted under Section 5 of this Act, for the purpose of providing medical or pharmaceutical care for their patients or for reviewing information regarding prescriptions that are recorded as having been issued or dispensed by the requester.

II. A patient who requests the patient's own prescription monitoring information, or of the parent or legal guardian of a minor child, in accordance with procedures established under [insert state statute granting individuals access to state held information concerning themselves].

III. [Insert name or type of state boards and regulatory agencies that supervise or regulate a profession that is authorized for controlled substances or other drug required to be submitted under Section 5 of this Act activity] if the request is pursuant to an investigation or is pursuant to the agency's official duties and responsibilities.

IV. Local, state and federal law enforcement or prosecutorial officials engaged in the administration, investigation or enforcement of the laws governing controlled substances or other drug required to be submitted under Section 5 of this Act pursuant to the agency's official duties and responsibilities.

V. [Insert state Medicaid agency's unit(s) with legal authority to conduct investigations and utilization review of program services] regarding Medicaid program recipients or Medicaid program providers.

VI. [Insert titles of medical examiners, coroners or others authorized under law to investigate causes of deaths] for cases under investigation pursuant to their official duties and responsibilities.

VII. Personnel of the [designated state agency] for purposes of administration and enforcement of this Act, or [insert state controlled substances act], [if any other state statute is applicable, insert "or" and reference the other statutes].

[Note: A state may determine to authorize additional agencies to request and receive prescription information including substance abuse treatment providers, worker's compensation board reviewers who are health care professionals, drug court judges, department of corrections' health care professional staff, and probation departments, if they cannot receive information under other provisions already authorized in (I) through (VII)]

(c) The [designated state agency] may provide information to public or private entities for statistical, research, or educational purposes after encrypting or removing the patient name, street name and number, patient ID number, and month and day of birth that could be used to identity individual patients and/or persons who received prescriptions from dispensers.

[Note: A state may choose to further restrict information released to researchers by encrypting or removing information that could be used to identify a prescriber, a pharmacy, or any other person.]

With this Model Act as the foundation, the following changes are indicated:

1. **Prescribers: proactive (unsolicited) reports** -- Some PMPs proactively analyze their databases and, when they identify probable doctor shoppers, they send an unsolicited report to the prescribers. Experience

indicates such reports result not only in reducing the subsequent prescriptions obtained by the doctor shoppers but also in a significant increase in prescribers requesting solicited PMP data and in a general reduction in prescriptions to doctor shoppers, even those for whom no report is sent out. We need to increase PMP use of unsolicited reports by:

a) Automating PMP analysis by developing algorithms that can be computer applied and validated.
b) Automating unsolicited reports by sending out alerts by email or by computer generated letters that advise prescribers that they have been prescribing to a person who may be a doctor shopper and informing the prescriber how they can access the information regarding this person. Several PMPs are working to develop this capability.
c) Automating follow-up, including tracking of prescriptions received by the probable doctor shopper subsequent to the unsolicited reports.

2. **Prescribers: requested (solicited) reports** - Upon request, PMPs provide prescription histories to prescribers so they can make clinically sound decisions prior to issuing prescriptions for controlled substances and can avoid being duped by doctor shoppers. This is generally done by PMPs providing web-portals through which prescribers may request data. We need to increase prescriber use of PMPs through:

a) Making data more timely – in April, the Oklahoma PMP began collecting data from pharmacies at point of sale; we need to expand this to all PMPs.
b) Making access seamless – Massachusetts PMP is moving to make its PMP interoperable with Electronic Health Records so prescribers can access the PMP from a single EHR sign-on; we need to expand this to all PMPs.
c) Combing PMPs and e-Prescribing of Controlled Substances – PMPs should become interoperable with e-Prescribing systems so:

I. Obtaining of an e-prescribing certification for controlled substances should be accepted by PMPs as authentication for access to PMP data.
II. As prescribers enter the name of a controlled substance drug for e-prescription, the patient's controlled substances history from the PMP pops up on their electronic device.
III. iii. As each e-prescription is sent to a pharmacy, a copy should be routed to the PMP database.

IV. iv. As each e-prescription is dispensed, the PMP should match the pharmacy's dispensing record to the corresponding e-prescription from the physician to identify any alterations and, if any, report to the appropriate agency.

d) Considering with public and private third party payers the value of mandating prescribers to access PMP data prior to issuing the first controlled substance prescription and periodically thereafter, as a condition of payment.

I. Reimbursement to prescribers for any additional time will need to be considered.

II. If such is required, third party payers will need automated assurance from the PMP that the prescriber accessed the PMP.

III. As provided in the Office of National Drug Control Policy's new Prescription Drug Abuse Prevention Plan, the PMP Center of Excellence is planning a meeting with third party payers and PMPs for 2011; this subject will be explored at the meeting.

3. **Pharmacies: requested (solicited) reports and proactive (unsolicited) reports** -- It is imperative for pharmacists to request and review PMP data prior to dispensing prescriptions for controlled substances.

a) The interoperability of PMPs with Electronic Health Records should include providing data to pharmacies in the manner described above for prescribers.
b) The e-Prescribing of Controlled Substances should include the PMP interoperability described above.
c) PMPs should forward proactive (unsolicited) reports to pharmacists, just as to prescribers.

4. **Pharmacies: verifications prior to dispensing** – In addition to the above, automated systems need to be designed to assure that controlled substances prescriptions are only dispensed after appropriate verification that requirements have been met. For example, should mandatory prescriber education be established (which the Center strongly supports), the list of trained prescribers should be automatically checked before a prescription is dispensed. The factors identified in the 2009 GAO report should be reviewed prior to dispensing, including verification that the prescriber is currently licensed and registered with DEA, has no licensure or registration restrictions that would affect controlled substances prescribing, and is not deceased.

Likewise, patients known to be deceased should not be allowed to have prescriptions dispensed in their names. Pharmacies will need to be properly compensated for this new work.

5. **Law Enforcement Agencies** – Local, state and federal Law Enforcement agencies and investigators are essential users of PMP data. This can be seen in the relatively lower death rates of unintentional opioid deaths in California, New York and Texas, i.e. these states have a long history of providing PMP solicited reports and unsolicited reports to investigators with law enforcement authority. Increased use of PMP data by law enforcement is essential if we are to going to impede the prescription drug abuse epidemic. We need to increase PMP use by law enforcement by:

a) Encouraging states to adopt policies that permit and encourage use of PMP data by law enforcement investigators.
b) Updating state PMP systems to automate law enforcements' approved access to the PMP data.

6. **Health Professional Licensing Agencies** – Agencies such as State Medical Boards and State Pharmacy Boards need ready access to PMP data to investigate potential misconduct and inappropriate use of controlled substances, e.g. self-abuse, over prescribing, and offering drugs to solicit sexual favors. Likewise, PMPs need to analyze their data and forward unsolicited reports to licensing boards when patterns of possible misconduct are found. This process needs to be automated to the extent feasible.

7. **Other users of PMP data** – If the expansion of the prescription drug abuse epidemic is to be slowed and reduced, then other parties need to have access to PMP data. Some states permit some of the parties below to have access, but this needs to be regularized and expanded across the nation:

a) State's Medicaid agency's unit(s) with legal authority to conduct investigations and utilization review of program services regarding Medicaid program recipients or Medicaid program providers.
b) Appropriate Medicare personnel.
c) Medical examiners, coroners or others authorized under law to investigate causes of deaths for cases under investigation pursuant to their official duties and responsibilities.
d) Substance abuse treatment providers.
e) Worker's compensation board reviewers who are health care professionals.

f) Drug court judges.
g) Department of corrections' health care professional staff, and probation departments, (if they cannot receive information under law enforcement provisions).
h) The Indian Health Services, Veterans Administration, and Department of Defense health care system (not just their prescribers but also the health care clinical supervisors who oversee prescribing and dispensing within those systems).
i) Health care systems' peer review organizations in order to identify and intervene in prescriber and pharmacist over-prescribing and miss-prescribing as early as possible, i.e. before the practices rise to the level that licensure or law enforcement action are required.
j) Other third party payers' health professional care reviewers - this is not currently being done and will require careful design to protect all data, but given the nature and extent of the epidemic, it appears unwise not to develop means by which PMPs and other third party payers can meaningfully exchange information.

8. **Early Warning System** – Pioneering work by the Massachusetts Department of Public Health's PMP and the principal investigator at the Center has identified an important new function for PMP data. Using spatial analysis methodology to examine Massachusetts PMP data when the drug OxyContin was introduced and subsequent years, a rapid expansion of doctor shopping can be seen, beginning in the first year, 1996. Review of data for 2005, shows that doctor shopping for all opioids had become widespread across the state and was concentrated most heavily in five geographic areas. A geospatial comparison to hospital data on opioid overdoses and opioid related deaths shows the same five areas had the highest rates of overdoses and deaths. Had this analysis been possible in prior years, the MA PMP could have issued warnings before the overdoses and deaths became epidemic. Warnings could be sent to all community, state and national stakeholders including health care practitioners, law enforcement, education, substance abuse prevention and treatment organizations, schools, parent teacher organizations, religious organizations and other groups. We must learn from this and assure that this does not happen again. We need to:

a) Fully develop the early warning methodology at the Center by obtaining data from other states that have already agreed to participate in a pilot development.

b) After development, provide the methodology to those states that are equipped to do the analyses.
c) Provide a service for those states not equipped to do their own analysis, i.e. the states can forward de-identified/encrypted PMP data to the Center so we can apply the methodology and return analyzed reports to them.
d) Compile analyzed information at the Center in order to produce regional and national warning information as changes emerge.

9. Concerns for youth – In response to Surgeon General Regina Benjamin's initiative to examine prescription drug abuse among youth, the Center has worked with the Maine, South Carolina and Wyoming PMPs to examine prescribing and doctor shopper patterns. The data indicates an increase in youth who are obtaining opioid prescriptions, during and after high school. Most surprisingly, the Wyoming data on doctor shoppers shows that peak of doctor shopping is among those aged 30 to 39, with a very large number 29 and younger. This represents a drop in age of almost two decades for those most actively involved in doctor shopping, compared with earlier research. This serves as a call for us to analyze PMP data from many states as rapidly as possible and, if the pattern holds up in other states, to get the word out widely. The nation's efforts to curtail youthful abuse of prescription drugs may need to add a new focus on stemming doctor shopping and other forms of prescription diversion among younger persons.

10. Mandatory Prescriber Education – A majority of prescribers have insufficient training in the use of opioids and other prescription controlled substances to safely prescribe these drugs. Such education needs to include training in not only the proper use of the drugs but also the misuse of, abuse of, and addiction to these drugs by bona fide patients; the nature and extent of doctor shopping; the extent of theft, counterfeiting and forgery of a prescribers' prescription pads; and how to access and use PMP data. As noted above, such training should not only be required but technologically monitored by pharmacies prior to dispensing. In addition, PMPs should periodically review their databases to assure that prescribers were trained at the time their prescriptions were dispensed; non-compliance should be proactively reported by the PMP to DEA and the state professional licensing agency.

INDEX

D

R

S

T

U

V

W

Y